A PORTRAIT OF CHARLES LAMB

Charles Lamb
1819.

TO RACHEL TRICKETT

There is no excellent beauty that has not
some strangeness in the proportion

FRANCIS BACON

A PORTRAIT OF CHARLES LAMB

BY

DAVID CECIL

CHARLES SCRIBNER'S SONS
NEW YORK

First American edition published 1984. Printed in Great Britain.

1 3 5 7 9 11 13 15 17 19   I/C   20 18 16 14 12 10 8 6 4 2

Library of Congress Catalog Card Number 84-51157
ISBN 0-684-18226-2
Picture research and design by John Hadfield

The portrait of Charles Lamb on the half-title page is from a watercolor drawing by G. F. Joseph, A.R.A., 1819 (British Museum Print Room).

The frontispiece is a detail from a Panorama of London, c. 1810, known as the "Rhinebeck" Panorama first published by the London Topographical Society in 1981.

CONTENTS

PART ONE

PART TWO

PART THREE

The quotations from letters by Charles and Mary Lamb are taken from the editions edited by E.V. Lucas, first published in 1912, and re-issued in 1935 by J.M. Dent & Sons Ltd., and Methuen & Company Ltd.

PART ONE

FLEET STREET: aquatint in J.B. Papworth's *Select Views of London*, 1816. Charles Lamb was born and lived for his early years within a few hundred yards of the original Temple Bar, which is in the background of this view.

CHAPTER I: CHILDHOOD

[1]

Charles Lamb, especially in his later years and when retired from his profession, disliked getting up early. As he explained to the world in an essay he wrote under the assumed name of Elia, he was not taken with the idea of rising with the lark:

> At what precise minute that little airy musician doffs his night gear and prepares to tune up his unseasonable matins we are not naturalists enough to determine. But for a mere human gentleman – that has no orchestra business to call him from his warm bed to such preposterous exercises – we take ten, or half after ten (eleven, of course, during this Christmas solstice) to be the very earliest hour at which he can begin to think of abandoning his pillow. To think of it, we say; for to do it in earnest requires another half hour's good consideration . . . Why should we get up? We have neither suit to solicit, nor affairs to manage. The drama has shut us up at the fourth act. We have nothing here to expect, but in a short time a sick-bed, and a dismissal. We delight to anticipate death by such shadows as night affords. We are already half acquainted with ghosts. We were never much in the world. Disappointment early struck a dark veil between us and its dazzling illusions. Our spirits showed grey before our hairs. The mighty changes of the world already appear as but the vain stuff out of which dramas are composed . . . We once thought life to be something; but it has unaccountably fallen from us before its time. Therefore we choose to dally with visions. The sun has no purposes of ours to light us to. Why should we get up?

The state of mind made articulate in this passage is a curious mixture. Starting in an easy, homely, comfortable tone – though lit up by a flicker of playful fantasy – it then modulates unexpectedly and imperceptibly into a wilder, sadder strain. Lying at rest in bed associates itself in the author's mind with lying at rest in the grave; taking refuge in his bedroom from the rush of active life outside, he sees himself also as taking refuge from the harsh disillusioning realities of human existence. Thus, melancholy and a hint of eerie fear steal in to mingle with the playfulness. Yet they do not expel it; Lamb's smile remains, though touched for a moment with wistfulness, as if half amused by his own darker fancies; so that – it would seem deliberately – he leaves his readers to decide how seriously they should take them.

[11]

This ambiguous blend of mood and thought is a distinguishing characteristic of Charles Lamb's personality; also of his life-story. His origins were relatively humble. John Lamb, his father, started work as a liveried servant, rose to be a scrivener, and finally established himself in middle life in the employment of Samuel Salt, a respected ex-Member of Parliament and a Master of the Inner Temple. Salt was a large, vague, kindly man to whom John Lamb acted as a general factotum, at one moment his personal attendant helping him to adjust his clothes, at another his confidential secretary advising him about his legal business. John Lamb's wife came from a family in Hertford-shire where her widowed mother, Mrs. Field, still lived as housekeeper and caretaker at Blakesware, one of the great country houses of the neighbourhood. The Lambs had seven children of which only three survived infancy: John born in 1764, Mary in 1765, and ten years later Charles. The family, together with an unmarried sister of John Lamb, packed themselves into a set of chambers next to those inhabited by John Lamb's patron Samuel Salt at No. 2 Crown Office Row, Inner Temple, a house facing the wrought iron gates that opened on the green lawns of its garden. They formed a group of personalities as diverse and quaint and idiosyncratic as characters in a novel by Dickens. John Lamb was a clever, animated little figure, who, in addition to working very hard for his patron, occupied his superfluous energies with skill and success in a number of different ways: writing humorous verses, modelling figures in plaster, brewing punch, taking a hand at cribbage and, when he felt the need for some fresh air, angling and playing bowls. He was an attractive character in whom a generous impulsive temper contended at times with a naif reverence for the accepted forms and usages of society. Once, when he saw a gentleman of quality insulting a lady, he seized his sword from him and pummelled him with its hilt till he stopped. The next day he felt bound to apologise to him for treating a man of rank disrespectfully – though apparently without promising not to behave in the same way should the same situation arise.

Mrs. Lamb, from the little we know about her, was a contrast to her husband. Tall and stately, and with a look of Mrs. Siddons, the most famous tragedienne of the day, she was noted for the fact that her manners were very much those of a gentlewoman, a phrase implying something more formal and elaborate than was common in the world she lived in. This differentiated her from her sister-in-law Sarah, nicknamed Aunt Hetty, an eccentric, odd-tempered spinster, who took little part in household activities but spent her time in religious exercises, attending services and reading pious books. The exact nature of her faith is obscure; for, whereas she preferred to worship at a Unitarian Chapel where Christ was regarded as no more than an exceptionally holy man, her favourite manual of devotion was *The Imitation of Christ*, which centres around the belief that He was God Incarnate. For the rest she was outspoken to the point of tactlessness, but, as so often with tactless persons, was easily offended by the remarks of others. On the other hand, and perversely, she disliked her sister-in-law's ladylike manners, which she considered insincere. Anxious to placate her, Mrs. Lamb became more polite than ever; in consequence Aunt Hetty grew all the more convinced of her insincerity. Not unnaturally Mrs. Lamb took a dislike to Aunt Hetty. The tension between the two became a permanent and disturbing element in the domestic atmosphere at No. 2 Crown Office Row.

The two elder children also were noticeably different from each other. John Lamb junior, tall and handsome like his mother, was active, combative and not especially affectionate; short plain Mary was full of heart, home-loving, with literary interests and a delicate nervous system. The two were alike only in that each, in his or her way, was unlike the ordinary run of human beings; more first-hand in their views, more independent in their judgments. In this they were like their father and aunt: an incurable independence of spirit was characteristic of the Lamb family. This made its members unusually interesting. But at a price: it went along with a more sinister strain in their make-up. Many of the Lambs were unbalanced and some in the past had been mad. Whether or not the children were aware of it, there hung over them, now faint now darker, the shadow of insanity.

Little Charles was as unusual as the rest of the family. More like Mary than John, he was thoughtful, home-loving, tender-hearted; a small skinny shrimp of a child with delicate aquiline features and eyes and skin so dark as to give him an oriental look – had the Lambs Jewish blood? people wondered – and spindly legs that made him walk weakly and flat-footedly. He was also afflicted with a stutter, a sign that, again like his sister, he had an unusually high-strung nervous temperament. This made him more open than most people to intense feelings of fear and melancholy. As a compensation he had a fanciful exuberant imagination with which to entertain himself, an impish sense of fun and a warm evident sweetness of disposition which enabled him easily to make friends.

The circumstances of his upbringing were such as to bring out the different strains in his make-up. Since he was younger by ten years than the rest of his family, his early life was that of an only child, and at times a solitary one. His parents seem to have played little part in it. His father was too much occupied, his mother, though kindly enough, was too distant; her eldest son was the only one of her children that she cared much about. Young John, a vigorous growing male in his 'teens, could hardly be expected to take much interest in his child brother. However, Charles did not suffer from lack of love, for he got enough to furnish a whole family from his sister Mary. By nature affectionate, but not meeting with much response from parents or elder brother, she turned her whole capacity for love on to Charles. At once weakly and responsive, he was a natural object of affection to any soft-hearted person. But it cannot have been long before it was apparent that she was also drawn to him by an affinity of spirit rare even between brother and sister: by an extraordinary likeness in tastes, interests and nervous temperament. There were some differences between them: Mary was quieter and shyer than Charles and far less fanciful. But these differences only added the charm of strangeness to the pleasure she took in his company. In consequence, she devoted herself to him with a love that, because she was so much older than him, was reinforced by a maternal tenderness and sense of responsibility. Unwearied and delighted, she sympathised with him in his joys and comforted him in his sorrows, played with him, listened to him, took him for walks, told him stories, read to him and taught him very early to read to himself. Charles responded to her with equal ardour. Their devotion to one another grew and continued through the years to inspire what was to be by far the most important relationship in either of their lives.

Someone else in No. 2 Crown Office Row was especially fond of Charles. Unexpectedly, he touched a soft spot in the heart of his eccentric Aunt Hetty. Turning away from her religious exercises, she began to take notice of him, engaged him in long conversations and fed him with cakes that she had baked for his pleasure. Charles appreciated her attentions: as a child he was fonder of her than of the parents who noticed him so little. He enjoyed her cakes – food was always to be one of his chief pleasures – and was interested by her talk. This was much concerned with religion. Christian piety first

THE WITCH OF ENDOR:
engraving in Thomas Stackhouse's
New History of the Holy Bible,
1737 – 'that detestable picture,' as
Lamb described it in his essay on
'Witches and Other Night Fears'

presented itself to Charles Lamb in Unitarian terms as a matter of
benevolent feelings rather than of doctrinal truth. The thought of
these beautiful, benevolent feelings stirred his childish heart and he
tried to act in accordance with them, not always with success. Once,
walking across London Bridge with a particularly delicious piece of
Aunt Hetty's cake in his hand, he was accosted by a grey-headed,
smooth-tongued beggar man who asked him for alms. On an impulse
of what he hoped was Christian feeling, Charles gave him his cake.
Before he had got to the end of London Bridge, came a reaction.

> I burst into tears [he recalled later] thinking how ungrateful I had
> been to my good aunt, to go and give her good gift away to a
> stranger that I had never seen before, and who might be a bad man
> for aught I knew; and then I thought of the pleasure my aunt
> would be taking in thinking that I – I myself, and not another –

would eat her nice cake – and what should I say to her the next time I saw her – how naughty I was to part with her pretty present – and the odour of that spicy cake came back upon my recollection, and the pleasure and the curiosity I had taken in seeing her make it, and her joy when she sent it to the oven, and how disappointed she would feel that I had never had a bit of it in my mouth at least – and I blamed my impertinent spirit of alms-giving, and out-of-place hypocrisy of goodness, and above all I wished never to see the face again of that insidious, good-for-nothing, old grey imposter.

Thus, early in his life, Charles Lamb learnt that a virtuous impulse can lead to unforeseen and ironical consequences.

Indeed, and in more ways than one, Aunt Hetty caused him pain as well as pleasure. Her countenance was unprepossessing: withered, shrivelled, and given to unaccountable grimacing and muttering. On one occasion it gave him cause for alarm. He had discovered two volumes in his father's book closet, one a treatise on witches and their malignant practices, and the other a collection of Bible stories containing a picture of the Witch of Endor calling up the ghost of the prophet Samuel. A few nights later he woke up feeling frightened and went into the next room. What was his horror to be met with the sight of Aunt Hetty sitting up with her eyes shut, muttering unintelligibly and looking all too like the picture of the Witch of Endor in his father's book! The thought ran chillingly through him that Aunt Hetty was possibly a witch and that she was engaged in saying the Lord's Prayer backward which, according to the treatise on witch-craft, was what witches did when preparing to cast an evil spell. He stole back to bed to spend the rest of the night half-sleepless with terror. Next day in the cheerful light of morning he met Aunt Hetty looking friendly and her old self, and his fears began to fade. But he could not get them completely out of his head. They came back at night and continued to do so in the nights that followed, though with gradually lessening force. Several weeks passed, however, before he had completely convinced himself that Aunt Hetty was not a witch.

Alas, this conviction did not ensure him undisturbed nights! Alone and in the dark, the child Charles Lamb suffered appallingly from night fears, so much so that between the ages of four and eight, unless he knew that some comforting grown-up was near him, he was always liable to fancy, lying in bed, that some dreadful apparition – witch or ghost or hideous monster – had settled silently behind him on his pillow, freezing his blood with fear. Even next morning if he went into his bedroom he turned instinctively towards the window and away from the bed lest, at the sight of the pillow, his fears might begin unbidden to reawaken. The truth was that, like many hyper-sensitive persons, Lamb felt at times inexplicably insecure, attacked by an obscure sense of terror that embodied itself to his imagination in some figure of terror that he had read about. Since his imagination was unusually strong, these figures were unusually and disagreeably vivid.

All the same, and in spite of some bad nights, he had a happy childhood: and by means of the same imagination that inspired his fears. It was all the more active because he was often alone; even the devoted Mary had only limited time to spend with him. He had to amuse himself. This he did by telling himself stories, playing pretend-games of his own invention, making up delightful thrilling fantasies. He drew the material for these from many sources. Much of it came from books. He had access to a great many, for Samuel Salt had a library and had given the Lamb children the run of it. Charles took full advantage of this. Novels, plays, poems, even history books – he had a look at them all – and, though understanding only a small proportion of what he read, managed to extract plenty to excite his fancy. From the first it seems that anything connected with the past had a special charm for him. He delighted in faded prints depicting outmoded costumes and discontinued picturesque customs; he could absorb himself in half-understood old tales about the adventures of comic rogues and glamorous princes and princesses. The fact that these were often written in strange, archaic language added to their charm. Charles was the kind of child who enjoys words; odd and unfamiliar ones especially appealed to him.

When he was six years old his imagination received a fresh and different stimulus. He had a godfather, also called Field, who kept an oil shop close to Drury Lane Theatre, which he supplied with oil for its orchestra lamps. In return, Mr. Sheridan – father of the author of *The School for Scandal* – who usually found it inconvenient to pay for the oil, would instead present Mr. Field from time to time with free tickets for the theatre. One evening in 1781 he made use of these to invite the Lamb family to attend a performance as his guests. Charles for the first time was included in the party; he arrived at Drury Lane tense with excitement, and all the more because at one moment the weather had looked as if it might be too rainy for the Lambs to risk the walk from the Temple to Drury Lane. Previous anxiety, however, only increased Charles's exhilaration when, at last safe in his seat, he gazed around the festive scene: gilded cornices, glittering chandeliers, gleaming glass pilasters – Charles thought these were made of sugar candy – beautiful ladies of fashion rustling and murmuring in the side boxes. Overcome with excitement he buried his face in his mother's lap till the rise of the curtain. The piece was *Artaxerxes*, a tragedy about a king of ancient Persia. Charles had read something about ancient Persia in a history book, enough for its name to evoke in his mind vague, gorgeous, exotic pictures. What a thrill it was for him to find these pictures translated into reality, actually to see before his eyes the palace of Persepolis, its temples and their altars smoking with a sacred flame, and, moving among them to the strains of solemn music, the splendidly costumed figures of the Persian monarch and his courtiers! Charles could not follow much of what was happening; but this did not matter; the spectacle was enough. Nor was it the only spectacle shewn him on that memorable evening. Playgoers expected their moneysworth in those days and the tragedy was followed by a pantomime. Harlequin, Columbine and Pantaloon now sprang forward to posture and pirouette before the grave and enthralled gaze of the six-year-old Charles. Though the pantomime was intended as light relief after the tragedy, to his innocent eye it was just another glorious example of gripping drama. He left Drury Lane a confirmed playgoer for life; and with his spirit furnished with new fuel to kindle his fantasies to flame.

They were also fired by the surroundings in which he lived. To anyone with a feeling for the historic past the Temple buildings were alive with romantic associations: the round church with its massive Norman pillars and grotesque medieval carvings, the timbered Elizabethan Dining Hall, the classic courts echoing with plash of water from sculptured fountains, the green garden with its mossy trees and time-blurred sundials, where little Charles used to play in the mornings. Some of the people he saw there impressed him as much as their surroundings did. Looking up from play he would gaze with awe at the venerable figures of the elderly Benchers of the Inner Temple strolling sedately across the smooth lawns. He learned to recognise some of them: formidable Mr. Thomas Coventry with his elephant-like gait and red waistcoat sprinkled with grains of snuff, thin Mr. Wharry with his curious walk – three steps and then a little jump – Mr. Mingey who talked in loud blustering tones and had a hook instead of a right hand, kindly Samuel Salt himself, the family's friend and patron. Perhaps because his father spoke of them with reverence these figures were, in the little boy, invested with a mysterious grandeur, as of beings almost supernatural. Recalling them years later he said with amusement: 'In those days I saw Gods as old men covered with mantles walking upon the earth.'

Infirm old gentlemen in the costumes of the late Georgian period would seem odd incarnations of Divinity. But things did not have to be obviously romantic to spark off Lamb's imagination; nor, for all his

Opposite: THE TEMPLE CHURCH, aquatint by J. Bluck after Pugin and Rowlandson in Ackermann's *Microcosm of London*, Volume I, 1805

feeling for the past, did they need to be antique. On the contrary it could equally take fire from the world and age he had been born into. Just outside the tranquil Temple Courts roared and seethed the life of contemporary London, rough and full-blooded, crude and colourful. Lamb found himself plunged into the midst of it as soon as he stepped out of the Temple precincts to accompany Mary out shopping or to be shepherded by her on his way to the little school in Fetter Lane, Holborn, where he learned some of his first lessons. With delight and excitement he responded to the bustle and noise of the scene and its various incidents: troops marching, hawkers crying their wares, boy chimney-sweeps with their brooms and black faces and gleaming white grins, gaudy inn signs creaking in the wind, and all the motley throng of people crowding and jostling their way through streets and narrow alleys. Here was yet more stuff to feed his imagination!

[III]

Now and again his life was varied by a visit to the country to stay in Hertfordshire with his maternal grandmother Mrs. Field at Blakesware, where she was caretaker, or with his great aunt Mrs. Gladman at her husband's farm at Mackery End. Mackery End gave him his first glimpse of rural life. He took a normal child's pleasure in observing the antics of the chickens in the poultry yard or in helping to collect eggs or to pick bunches of sweet-smelling wild violets growing in the hedges around the farm. But these country delights did not mean much to Charles. They lacked the human interest needed to contribute to the fantasy life which was the centre and mainspring of his childhood existence. Not so Blakesware. Blakesware might have been created to stir Lamb's fancy: more even than the Temple did it stimulate his feeling for the romance of past ages. Every plank and

Opposite: INNER TEMPLE COURT: coloured aquatint by Thomas Malton in *A Picturesque Tour through the Cities of London and Westminster*, 1792

panel of it, he said, had magic for him. In particular a visit he paid there in the fine summer of 1782, when he was seven years old, was a landmark in the history of his imaginative life. Blakesware was a spacious mansion built in 1640; and, because its owners had not made their main home there, hardly altered since then. Mrs. Field lived comfortably in what had been designed as quarters for the upper servants. Charles used to recall with Proustian vividness happy mornings curled up in the sunny window seat of her store-room absorbed in a volume of Cowley's poems, the words and rhythms mingling in his memory with the summer warmth, the buzz of a wasp in the window pane and the fresh green of the grass which met his eyes when he raised them from the page to glance outside. But his most precious memories were of his wanderings through the great rooms of the mansion: the hall ornamentated with prints after *The Rake's* and *Harlot's Progress* by Hogarth – little Charles gazed at these with mingled amusement and horror – and busts of the Roman Emperors, the corridors and drawing rooms with their marbles and gilt furniture and family portraits, the state bedrooms hung with tapestry and with majestic canopied beds. The fact that the house was not lived in increased its compelling power over his imagination; for it enabled him all the better to people it with picturesque ghosts, imagined figures of its past inhabitants. He learned about them from his grandmother, a stately upright old lady in black who took pride in the family she served and loved, recounting their histories, and he knew their faces from their portraits: Caroline gentlemen in lovelocks, Restoration gallants in periwigs, and their satin-clad brides adorned with ringlets and pearl ear-drops – all of them disposed in attitudes of conscious grace against backgrounds of cloudy sky or pillared portico. One portrait held a special fascination for him, that of a fair-haired girl dressed as a shepherdess in pastoral blue and accompanied by a lamb; she established herself in his mind as his ideal of feminine beauty. It became one of his daydream games to pretend that Blakesware was his home, as it had been hers, and the Lambs also a

BLAKESWARE: watercolour drawing by H.G. Oldfield, c. 1800

family of rank, and himself their heir, the latest of a long line of
ancestors and with a coat of arms, complete with motto, to be
blazoned after his death on a scutcheon, like that which hung in
tattered state on the walls of Blakesware's Grand Staircase.

The spell cast on him by the house extended its power to the
grounds, the scene of his solitary roamings; sunlit lawns and clear fish
ponds and umbrageous groves providing yet another setting for
enchanted flights of fancy. These blissful summer days at Blakesware
made a unique, indelible impression on Charles's memory, that was
more than once, years later, exquisitely to inspire his art:

> It was an old deserted place, yet not so long deserted but that
> traces of splendour of past inmates were everywhere apparent. Its
> furniture was still standing – even to the tarnished gilt leather

battledores and crumbling feathers of shuttlecocks in the nursery, which told that children had once played there. But I was a lonely child, and had the range at will of every apartment, in every nook and corner, wondered and worshipped everywhere. . . In particular I used to spend many hours by myself, in gazing upon the old busts of the Twelve Caesars that had been Emperors of Rome, till the old marble heads would seem to live again, or I to be turned into marble with them; how I never could be tired with roaming about the huge mansion, with its vast empty rooms, with their worn-out hangings, fluttering tapestry and carved oaken panels, with the gilding almost rubbed out – sometimes in the spacious old-fashioned gardens, which I had almost to myself, unless when now and then a solitary gardening man would cross one – and how the nectarines and peaches hung upon the walls, without my ever offering to pluck them, because they were forbidden fruit, unless now and then – and because I had more pleasure in strolling about among the old melancholy-looking yew trees, or the firs, and picking up the red berries and the fir apples, which were good for nothing but to look at – or in lying about upon the fresh grass with all the fine garden smells around me – or basking in the orangery, till I could almost fancy myself ripening too along with the oranges and limes in that grateful warmth – or in watching the dace that darted to and fro in the fishpond, at the bottom of the garden, with here and there a great sulky pike hanging midway down in the water in silent state, as if it mocked at their impertinent friskings, – I had more pleasure in these busy-idle diversions than in all the sweet flavours of peaches, nectarines, oranges, and such like common baits of children . . . The solitude of childhood is not so much the mother of thought, as it is the feeder of love, and silence, and admiration. So strange a passion for the place possessed me in those years, that, though there lay – I shame to say how few roads distant from the mansion – half hid by trees, what I judged some romantic lake, such was the spell that bound me to the house, and such my carefulness not to pass its strict and proper precincts, that the idle witness lay unexplored for me; and not till late in life, curiosity prevailing over elder devotion, I found, to my astonishment, a pretty brawling brook had been the Lacus Incognitus of my infancy. Variegated views, extensive prospects – and those at no great distance from the house – I was told of such – what were they to me, being out of the boundaries of my Eden? – So far from a wish to roam, I would have drawn, methought, still closer the fence of my chosen prison; and have been hemmed in by a yet securer cincture of those excluding garden walls.

It was to be noted that even at Blakesware Charles's feelings were never so rapturous as wholly to free him from fear. Blakesware might be an earthly paradise, but paradise he realised had bounds; bounds which he dared not cross for beyond them, he suspected, was danger – from witches or monsters or wicked people. Charles's reading had made him early aware of the existence of wicked people. Once, when he was a very little boy, Mary took him for a walk in the churchyard. He examined the inscriptions on the tombstones and was puzzled by the fact that they only mentioned the virtues of the persons commemorated, as if they had no faults worth speaking of. Charles paused and pondered: 'Mary, where are the naughty people?' he asked.

CHAPTER II: SCHOOLDAYS

Charles's goodbye to Blakesware that radiant summer may stand for his goodbye to childhood. Samuel Salt was a Governor of Christ's Hospital, and in gratitude to John Lamb for serving him so well used his influence to get the Lambs' sons into the school. In the autumn of 1782 therefore, and dressed in what had been the regulation dress ever since the school's foundation by the boy King Edward VI in the sixteenth century – yellow stockings, white neck-bands, leather-belted, heavily-skirted dark blue gown – the seven-year-old Charles left home to spend the next eight years of his life as a Blue-coat boy. This meant a formidable change in his life; and all the more because Christ's Hospital in the eighteenth century was a formidable place. It was so big, for one thing: over five hundred boys, their ages ranging from seven to seventeen, sat down to dinner every day in the Great Hall. Moreover life there presented such a mixture of splendours and miseries. Certainly it had its splendours: visual splendours as manifested in the arched and ancient cloisters, in the Great Hall lined with vast canvases painted by Lely and Verrio flamboyantly commemorating events in the school's history; in the traditional rituals like the solemn Easter procession through the streets of London to the Mansion House to be regaled with wine and buns by the Lord Mayor himself, or in the Christmas festivities with fireside feasts and carol singing. Intellectual splendours too; Christ's Hospital was not a Philistine institution. The six or seven senior scholars – they were known as Grecians and Deputy Grecians – were acknowledged by the boys as well as the masters to be the kings of the place: the best teachers were true men of learning; the cleverer boys responded to their teaching and in their turn stimulated and entertained each other. The fact that they lived in monastic seclusion, cut off from other boys by their dress and brief holidays, encouraged their common activities and intensified their feelings for each other. And it endued all members of the school with a strong corporate pride. Strangers noted

CHRIST'S HOSPITAL: engraving by Record, 1776

that their demeanour, though modest, as if aware that they were likely to be regarded as charity children, was yet marked by the inner confidence of those who believed that there was no school in England better than theirs, and few as good.

So much for the splendours. What about the miseries? By the standards of today these were considerable. Terms, though broken by a good many single holidays and half holidays, took up ten months of the year. During them the regime was severe: up at six in the summer and seven in the winter, followed by eight hours of work before bed, which was at seven for the younger boys and eight for the older. On Sundays they attended two lengthy services filled out with hour-long sermons during which they were vigilantly watched lest they should go to sleep. The strain of life at Christ's Hospital was not rendered easier by inefficient catering. The boys had little to eat, and what there was unappetising. Sometimes a meal consisted of no more than a chunk of stale bread washed down by a mug of stale beer. If anything more eatable was provided it was liable to be devoured by the school

BLUE-COAT BOYS DRAWING A LOTTERY AT COOPER'S HALL: detail from an aquatint by Stadler after Pugin and Rowlandson, in Ackermann's *Microcosm of London*, Volume II, 1809. In his 'Recollections of Christ's Hospital', 1813, Lamb referred to 'our solemn processions through the City at Easter, with the Lord Mayor's largess of buns, wine and a shilling, with the festive questions and civic pleasantries of the dispensing Alderman'. Blue-coat boys were obviously regarded as part of the City establishment.

servants before it reached the boys. Discipline, though mercifully not always well-kept, was at best strict and at worst savage. In class it was maintained by the masters, out of class by monitors called King's Boys, a section of tough youths destined to go to sea. The main punishment, used alike by boys and masters, seems to have been

flogging; it was employed freely, and by the King's Boys enthusiastically. At night in the dormitories some of these took advantage of any
pretext to entertain themselves by belabouring their trembling
juniors with leather belts. For the few crimes that the school looked on
as heinous the official punishments were horribly harsh. If a boy tried
to run away, for instance, he was chained up for hours on end in a
minute, dark dungeon; if he repeated the offence he was taken out
from it at intervals to be publicly scourged by a school official called
the beadle. If he persisted in trying to run away he was expelled after a
horrifying ceremony in which, dressed in some garment of disgrace
and in the presence of the whole school, he was subjected to a final
scourging before being publicly driven out of Christ's Hospital for
ever.

Altogether existence there presented growing boys with a startl-
ingly candid and forceful preview of life's potentialities alike for joy
and for suffering. How did Charles Lamb react to this? With mixed
feelings; he was far too sensitive for the sufferings not to leave a strong
impression on him. Never was he to forget the shock he felt, on his
arrival as a little child of seven, at the sight of a would-be runaway,
white-faced with terror, and fettered. Yet he was also to remember his
old school with reverence and affection and gratitude and to speak of
his time there as a peculiarly happy one. In fact he had to face the
darker side of Blue-coat life comparatively rarely and never as part of
his personal experience. His circumstances were such as to shield him
from it, while enjoying the satisfactions of Blue-coat life to the full.
The fact that he lived in the same house as one of the school's
governors, and under his patronage, meant that neither boys or
masters were likely to ill-treat him, lest he should complain of them.
More important, he was not cut off from home. The school was only
ten minutes walk from the Temple; so he was able to spend much of
his free time there, going back twice a week on half-holidays to relax
from the rigours and anxieties of school life, lounging in the garden,
endlessly reading in Mr. Salt's library, and talking and laughing with

Mary – also having a good meal. Even at school his home connection enabled him to be better fed than his companions, for Aunt Hetty often called on him, carrying a basket containing tea, fresh rolls and now and again a delicious slice of roast veal. Charles found it a little embarrassing when – looking presumably strange and witchlike – she sat herself down on some steps leading to the school coal hole and unpacked these delicacies before the eyes of his hungry school-fellows. Still, the delicacies were worth the embarrassment.

Nor is there any record that the school-fellows protested, for – and this more than anything else made his schooldays happy – they liked him too much. His weakness set him a little apart from the other boys: he was unable to share in their more strenuous sports and activities. Instead he passed much of his time wandering about by himself, absorbed in his reveries, and looking, it was said, like an earnest young monk. But there was something immediately likeable about his personality that led the other boys to be kind to him on account of his weakness, and disposed them to make friends with him. Gaily and readily he responded to their overtures. It was not long before they discovered that he was delightful as well as likeable – good-natured, sympathetic, and capable of infectious flights of fun and fancy which were accompanied by fits of wild laughter. Nor was he so fastidious as to be put off by schoolboy boisterousness and silliness. Indeed, though much above the average in brains, he had more in common with ordinary schoolboys than at first sight might appear. Like them, he was interested in his food, and in making fun of the masters. He shared their taste for tall stories, comical or bloodcurdling, delighted as they did in hoaxes and jokes – good or bad, it did not matter which. He was normal enough to be a comfortable companion to other boys and original enough to be an entertaining one. Gradually he grew to be the object of a special and amused affection. Indeed he must have been so from early days for it was noted that whereas other boys were known only by their surnames he was spoken of by everyone as Charles Lamb. He had been born with charm, and from the time he

A SCHOLAR OF CHRIST'S
HOSPITAL: aquatint in
Ackermann's *History of the Free-
School of Christ's Hospital*, 1816.
'Nor would I willingly forget any
of the things which administered
to our vanity. The hem-stitched
bands and town-made shirts,
which some of the most
fashionable among us wore: the
town-girdles, with buckles of silver
or shining stone, the badges of the
sea-boys; the cots, or superior
shoe-strings of the monitors; the
medals of the markers (those who
were appointed to hear the Bible
read in the wards on Sunday
morning and evening), which bore
on their obverse in silver, as
certain parts of our garments
carried in meaner metal, the
countenance of our founder, that
godly and royal child, King
Edward the Sixth, the flower of
the Tudor name – the young
flower that was untimely cropped'.
– Lamb's 'Recollections of Christ's
Hospital' in *The Gentleman's
Magazine*, 1813.

arrived at Christ's Hospital as an odd, stuttering seven-year-old it
made itself felt.

On his side, he felt at ease with his schoolfellows. He was
gregarious and, given that he had enough time alone in which to
indulge his private thoughts and fancies, he liked being in a crowd. He
liked it all the better for being a Blue-coat crowd. To feel himself
belonging to a famous and venerated institution, and buoyed up by its
confident corporate spirit, fortified him against any inclination to

shrink from life as something dangerous and uncharted and lonely.

Christ's Hospital also won his affection as appealing to his romantic sense of the past – by the fact that his dress was the same as that worn in the days of its sixteenth-century founder, that generations of previous scholars had dined in the historic Hall, idled in the ancient cloisters, marched in the Easter procession to the Mansion House. Always he was to recollect how, in his early days at school, as a little boy on Christmas Eve he had lain in bed in the dormitory listening to the ethereal distant voices of the choir boys below singing carols, and how he had thought that thus must have sounded the voices of the angels announcing the birth of the Saviour to the shepherds in the starlit fields outside Bethlehem on the first Christmas Eve. The Blue-coat boys got to know the Bible stories very well. As members of a religious foundation they followed the Christian year as it manifested itself in the traditional services and rituals, succeeding one another from Christmas to Advent. These, together with the magnificent antique language of the liturgy, further enriched Lamb's imaginative life. That of his school fellows too: their semi-monastic mode of living encouraged the growth of religious sentiment so that many became romantically pious, credulous of marvels and miracles. The taste for such things extended to their secular reading; it is not surprising that *The Arabian Nights* was among their favourite books.

Lamb got the same kind of pleasure from much of what he studied in class: the tales of the gods and heroes of ancient Greece and Rome also appealed to his sense of wonder and of the historic past. He was taught mainly by two masters, both clergymen, though by modern standards not very clerical. The first, the Reverend Matthew Field, was a handsome, easy-going man, elegantly dressed, with a taste for the theatre and not given to hard work. He often arrived after the hour appointed for lessons and left before that appointed for its close. Left to their own devices, the boys occupied themselves happily playing cat's cradle, constructing paper houses and reading *The Arabian Nights*. During such time as he did spend with them, Mr. Field sat

about looking genial and gentlemanly and absentminded. When asked a question he often answered in such a way as to show he had not listened to it. The boys took advantage of this. 'Are you not a great fool?' a pupil asked him. 'Yes, child,' vaguely replied the Reverend Mr. Field. His beatings – for even he felt bound to beat sometimes – amounted to no more than ceremonial tappings. Not so those of Lamb's other master, the Reverend James Boyer! A short stout figure with angry eyes and long upper lip, he was extremely irascible; he worked his pupils hard and if, as often happened, they failed to satisfy him, he beat them mercilessly. 'Poor old James Boyer,' remarked a former pupil on hearing of his death. 'May all his faults be forgiven and may he be wafted to bliss by little cherub boys all head and wings

and with no bottoms to reproach his sublunary infirmities.' There is a
touch of affection in the tone of this remark; and indeed the Reverend
Mr. Boyer was liked as well as feared. He was warm-hearted as well as
hot-tempered, and was an inspiring teacher. Homer and Catullus
were for him living authors in whom he delighted, and whom he was
able to make his pupils delight in too. What was rare in those days: he
also taught them about English literature, and in the same way
inspired them to enjoy Shakespeare and Milton. He encouraged
pupils to write themselves; and if he like the result he praised them as
readily as he had beaten them when they had displeased him. He kept
a volume in which, now and again, he inscribed pieces of original
writing which he thought particularly well of, composed by members
of the school. He once included a piece by Charles Lamb. Lamb was
the kind of pupil to learn a great deal from Boyer, who fostered his
appreciation of literature while at the same time disciplining his
methods of work. For this, and for the fun he got out of his
idiosyncracies, Lamb forgave Boyer for any beatings he may have
received at his hands.

Masters, however – whether inspiring or alarming – played a less
important and less influential part in Charles Lamb's school life than
did his contemporaries. Friendship throughout his life was a chief
source of his happiness, and it was at Christ's Hospital that he first
learned to make friends. Within a year or two of arriving at school we
hear of him as a member of a group made up of boys like himself,
literary, lively and with a gift for amusing themselves. Together they
occupied their spare time discussing, arguing, gossiping, writing light
verses, joking: they took a special and perhaps regrettable pleasure in
puns and vied with each other as to who could make the most
outrageous ones. Accounts of them and their doings gave a general
impression of active-minded, high-spirited youth from which fleetingly emerge some individual figures – handsome, laughing Bob
Allen; genial, stage-struck Jem White; and two brothers called Le
Grice; delicate-featured Sam, famous for his daring in cheeking his

school masters; and his elder brother Val – a particular friend of Charles Lamb – small, plump, humorous and with a turn for repartee much admired by his friends.

With them, but somehow apart from the rest, was to be observed a more striking figure, a pallid-faced boy with dark wavy hair, framing a noble brow and a pair of dreamy dilated eyes whose effect was slightly weakened by an indeterminate chin and soft-lipped mouth, generally half open as if its owner's breathing was obstructed by adenoids. Also by the fact that he was almost always talking. From his lips poured forth a flow of words delivered in expressive tones and which – though they could include puns and jokes – were more characteristically marked by a precocious depth of learning and a strain of high-flown poetic imagination. Samuel Taylor Coleridge was the son of a Devonshire vicar and three years older than Charles Lamb; but he came to Christ's Hospital in the same term. Though unpractical and undecided – the impression made by his chin was not deceptive – he early shewed signs of remarkable mental powers. During his first years as a Blue-coat boy these matured with dazzling speed. By fourteen years old he was already a magnetic personality marked by signs of original creative genius, pursuing his own lines of thought on philosophy and theology and literature; and he could talk about them in such a way as to enthral those who heard him. Visitors walking round the school cloisters would pause to gaze with surprised curiosity at the sight of a wide-eyed, unusual-looking boy surrounded by a cluster of school-fellows who listened spellbound as he discoursed to them ardently about the philosophy of Plotinus, or thrillingly declaimed passages from the works of Homer and Pindar. Lamb was one of the listeners. It is possible that in common with some others, then and later, he did not always understand what Coleridge was saying. But he understood enough to fall under his spell, to feel the pull of his magnetism. He was to feel it more strongly in the future. Getting to know Coleridge was to prove the most important event in Charles Lamb's school life.

CHAPTER III : CITY CLERK

[1]

The years passed and Lamb and his friends became in their turn Kings of the school. Lamb achieved the distinguished rank of Deputy Grecian. Usually the most scholarly Blue-coat boys were sent on to the university to be prepared for ordination. The school authorities judged that Lamb, though scholarly enough, stuttered too badly to be a clergyman. Two of the school governors, however, friends of Mr. Salt, interested themselves in his future. In consequence of their efforts he left Christ's Hospital in the winter of 1789 to become a temporary clerk in the service of Joseph Plaice, a City merchant. Lamb was not yet quite fifteen, an early age, it might seem, to join the ranks of London's hard-worked, grown-up wage-earners. But this change in his life was less hard on him than it might have been on some boys. For one thing Mr. Plaice's office was not far from the Temple; so he could still go on living at home with his family and was able in his free time to stroll round to Christ's Hospital for a talk with such friends as remained there. Except intellectually, Lamb was in many ways still childlike, and happy still to continue his childhood's way of life.

It might have been expected that this preference would have put him off grown-up work; all the more because it was not an especially congenial kind of work. Charles Lamb was not by nature a city clerk. But his very childishness helped him to adapt himself to his new role, for it was the childishness of a sweet-tempered, obedient, 'good' child with no impulse to rebellion but who accepted without much question the decrees of his elders and betters. Moreover, such a child readily

Opposite: THE HALL, BLUE-COAT SCHOOL: detail from aquatint by Hill after Pugin and Rowlandson in Ackermann's *Microcosm of London*, Volume I, 1808

submitted to the guidance of the persons set over him in his office; he wanted to please them and generally succeeded in doing so. For the rest, he had inner resources of enjoyment to fall back upon in the shape of his mental and imaginative life: in these he could always take refuge from any dullness of spirit induced by the drab realities of the daily round. It was true that this inner life brought with it anxieties. Lamb retained a child's vulnerability. His high-strung nervous system and high-pitched imagination still made him more liable than the average person to irrational terrors and fits of melancholy. Both at school and in the rough streets of eighteenth-century London he had, if only in glimpses, seen enough of brutal evil and suffering to keep alive his sense of human life as potentially dangerous: he partly clung to home because he felt safer there. Yet, at this stage in his story, these anxieties did not seem to have worried him unduly. He was young and hopeful and enjoyed himself enough to keep them at bay.

[11]

It took a little time for him to find permanent work. A year in Mr. Plaice's office was followed by another temporary job in the South Sea House. This was a stately old-fashioned leisurely place run by a handful of odd and elderly officials, whose habits and manners amused the boy clerk as much as had those of his school masters. From there, in April 1792, he made a final move to become an apprentice clerk in the Accounts Department of the East India Company in Leadenhall Street. He was to stay there for the rest of his working life. In other ways 1792 was to be an eventful year for Lamb.

Opposite: SOUTH-SEA HOUSE: detail from aquatint by Sutherland after Pugin and Rowlandson in Ackermann's *Microcosm of London*, Volume III, 1810. Lamb wrote: 'Here are still to be seen stately porticoes, imposing staircases, offices roomy as the state apartments in palaces – deserted, or thinly peopled with a few straggling clerks'.

In February Samuel Salt died. He left the Lamb family some money; this, added to their savings, ensured them a future which, though poor, was not poverty-stricken. All the same, Salt's death meant the loss of the family's patron and the break up of a long-established pattern of life; soon they would be making plans for leaving the house which had been their home so long.

Charles Lamb was also to remember 1792 for more romantic reasons. We do not know much about his romance – only what we can piece together from a few references in poems and letters. From these it appears that on a visit to his grandmother Field at Blakesware in the previous summer he had got to know a girl called Ann Simmons who was living in a cottage near the neighbouring village of Widford; also that she was gentle and timid, with fair hair and blue eyes and looked rather like the portrait of the girl with the lamb hanging on the walls of Blakesware which had embodied for him, ever since childhood, his ideal of feminine beauty. Now at seventeen years old, the correct age for first love, he duly fell in love with her. We are not told whether she returned his feelings. But she is unlikely to have appeared wholly unresponsive, since in later years he liked to recall happy walks with her through the green glades and winding woodland paths of the Hertfordshire countryside, his heart aglow with daydreams of eventually making her his wife. Alas, the relationship never got further than daydreams and country walks! Ann Simmons's family intervened firmly to discourage it. This is not surprising in view of the fact that Lamb was hardly more than a boy and, for the time being, a penniless boy: clerks were only paid a proper salary after the first three years of probation. As the year advanced circumstances changed still further to separate Lamb from his love. After he started work in April he hardly ever got long enough holidays to leave London; in August his grandmother Field died, which meant no more visits to Blakesware. In face of these obstacles his hopes began to fade. By the middle of the next year he speaks of Ann sadly but resignedly as one irretrievably lost to him. The tone in which he speaks, however,

EAST INDIA HOUSE, Leadenhall Street: drawn and engraved by Watts, 1800. This was where Lamb worked for thirty-three years.

suggests that he had not found resignation extremely difficult. Indeed his love had been no powerful mature passion, but rather the tentative, dreamy calf-love of a poetically-minded youth for a girl, chosen less for herself than because she seemed momentarily to incarnate a boyish ideal. Calf-love is a pretty sentiment, but too airborne and fanciful, too little rooted in reality, to be lasting.

Yet Lamb's love for Ann Simmons was to have a significance in his life story out of all proportion to its strength. For ever after, Ann, with her fair hair and tender blue-eyed glance, was to occupy a special and sanctified place in his recollections: as a middle-aged bachelor he was still to look back wistfully to his unrealised daydream of a happy home with her as his wife and the mother of his children, for – and this is what kept her image so much alive for him – no-one else was to take her place. She remained a unique figure in his life: fragile and unfulfilled as his feeling for her might seem, it was the only thing of its kind in his history, and his relation to her the nearest he ever got to a love affair.

Already there were grounds for suspecting that this might be so. Like Ann's relations, his grandmother Field had discouraged his thoughts of matrimony; but for more formidable reasons. He should

WIDFORD CHURCH: watercolour drawing by H.G. Oldfield, c. 1800. Less than a mile from Blakesware, Widford Church is where Lamb's maternal grandmother, Mary Field, the caretaker at Blakesware, was buried. Lamb often revisited Widford between 1827 and 1832, after his retirement from the East India Company, walking all the sixteen miles from Enfield.

not marry Ann, she told him, because this might lead to his propagating the Lamb family madness. This was equivalent to saying that he should never marry anyone. Even if he did not accept her view – and what he thought about it is yet another thing we do not know – he must have realised that it might be true and, as such, deeply disheartening. It made him instinctively hesitate before following the natural call of his heart and senses; it nipped in the bud any impulse he had wholeheartedly to fall in love. This was not very difficult: Charles Lamb was not a man of passion. But he had an unusual capacity for devoted affection. This, frustrated of other outlet, turned, from this time on, to pour itself out on those whom he had already learned to love: his family, his friends, above all his sister Mary. This was to have momentous consequences for him.

[III]

During the first years after he left school Lamb grew up. His disposition and taste had already disclosed themselves; now they matured to assume their permanent form. His disposition was contemplative. He had no wish to get things done, but rather to observe and reflect and weave fantasies. The nature of these contemplations was conditioned by the fact that he was by nature a hedonist, a man who fulfilled his nature by exercising an unusual gift for enjoying himself. As an observer, therefore, he was concerned less to note what struck him as important than what pleased him as beautiful or entertaining. Or loveable and touching, for Lamb – and here he differed from many hedonists – only enjoyed something intensely if it appealed to his heart as well as his sensibilities. 'All things are shadows to him,' Coleridge once said about him, 'except those that move his affections.'

These affectionate contemplations were not confined to the present and to the world he saw around him. The man Lamb, like the boy Lamb, lived largely in the past, the historic past as recorded in books and his own past as preserved in his memory. His inner life of memory and reflection was always a chief object of his attention. Averting his eyes from the outside world, he was fascinated to study the movements of his mind, to give rein to the flights of his imagination: unlike most men, he retained in manhood a child's capacity to live in a world of fantasy. He differed from a child, however, in recognising that his world of fantasy was not the world of reality, and he got a whimsical amusement out of this recognition. Over Lamb's prevailing mood flickered, often and unpredictably, a gleam of impish irony.

Such was his disposition. It coloured his attitude to his chief interests. The first of these was literature: reading was the centre and mainspring of his mental life, the source of his most exquisite pleasures. A pleasure not just passive but also creative, Lamb's literary taste – original, adventurous, little influenced by tradition – was a lively expression of an extremely individual personality. As such it had its limitations. Since he read only to be moved or amused, he felt no interest in books whose purpose was to inform and instruct, works of philosophy or science or serious history. Within its limits, however, his taste was remarkably wide: it embraced stories, plays, poems and essays; it could delight with equal relish in the realistic and the fantastic, in the tragic and the comic. In general he preferred old books to new; he liked his pleasures to be associated with his sense of the past. Thus he enjoyed the great eighteenth-century novels, *Moll Flanders* and *Tom Jones*, because they portrayed the crowded exuberant life of the London streets amid which he had grown up, and all the more attractively because they did it in slightly old-fashioned terms. Again, the literature of the sixteenth and seventeenth centuries appealed to Lamb's fanciful and poetic strain, and all the more because they spoke in accents that evoked the charm of a bygone and picturesque age. Partly for this reason, though he passionately admired its great accepted writers, Shakespeare and Milton, he got an almost equal gratification from other lesser-known contemporaries, poets like Donne, playwrights like Webster and Ford. These had

COVENT GARDEN THEATRE: aquatint by J. Bluck after Pugin and Rowlandson in Ackermann's *Microcosm of London*, Volume I, 1808

come to be neglected because the critics of later generations considered both their thoughts and their language grotesque and far-fetched. Lamb liked them all the better for these qualities. Furthermore, he took pleasure in feeling himself a pioneer in noting beauties long neglected. After all, many people in England already enjoyed reading a play by Shakespeare; but few, other than himself, enjoyed reading a play by Webster.

His pleasure in reading plays was reinforced by seeing them acted. It was seven years since he had been able to do this; for the Blue-coat boys were forbidden to go to the theatre. Now he made up for lost time. It did not cost him much: he could get a place on a bench in the upper gallery for two shillings; besides, now and again he was admitted on a free pass from his godfather Field. Lamb was soon a regular member of the audience at one or other of the two London theatres, Drury Lane and Covent Garden. At first he was disconcerted to find that he could no longer, as at seven years old, accept the performance as a reality: the scenes were all too obviously made of paint and pasteboard and the figures that moved among them rouged and costumed players. Soon however he learned to accept both as illusions; and discovered that, as such, they gave him an equal though different sort of satisfaction; satisfaction in the skill and intelligence with which a good performance imitated and interpreted and glorified reality. He had learned to enjoy the theatre not as reality but as art. Lamb was a born critic of the art of acting, readily responsive but always discriminating. Luckily this gift of his got every chance to exercise itself, for playgoing in these days coincided with a great period of English acting. Mrs. Siddons and Mrs. Jordan, John Kemble and Dodd, Munden and Dickie Suett, Bowley and Jack Bannister and Parsons – young Charles Lamb saw them all in their heyday and they made so deep an impression on him that thirty years later he could recall precisely the details of their performances in such a way as to convey them to us today, as when he speaks of Dodd as Sir Andrew Aguecheek:

> In expressing slowness of apprehension this actor surpassed all others. You could see the first dawn of an idea stealing slowly over his countenance, climbing up by little and little with a painful process, till it cleared up at last to the fulness of a twilight conception – its highest meridian. He seemed to keep back his intellect, as some have had the power to retard their pulsation. The balloon takes less time in filling than it took to cover the expansion of his broad moony face over all its quarters with expression. A glimmer of understanding would appear in a corner of his eye, and for lack of fuel go out again. A part of his forehead would catch a little intelligence, and be a long time in communicating it to the remainder.

or Mrs. Jordan as Viola speaking of her dead sister's concealed love:

JAMES DODD AS SIR ANDREW AGUECHEEK in *Twelfth Night*, Drury Lane, 1772:
detail from an engraving after a painting by Francis Wheatley. The part of Sir Toby
Belch was played by James Love.

MRS SIDDONS IN THE
CHARACTER OF LADY MACBETH:
détail from an engraving by C.
Rolls after a painting by G.H.
Harlow

It was no set speech, that she had foreseen so as to weave it into an harmonious period, line necessarily following line, to make up the music – yet I have heard it so spoken, or rather read, not without its grace and beauty – but, when she had declared her sister's history to be a 'blank', and that she 'never told her love', there was a pause, as if the story had ended – and then the image of the 'worm in the bud', came up as a new suggestion – and the heightened image of 'Patience' still followed after that, as by some growing (and not mechanical) process, thought springing up after thought. I would almost say, as they were watered by her tears.

Viola and Sir Andrew are figures in a comedy; and Lamb the playgoer was more wholly satisfied by comedy than tragedy, at least by the great Shakespearean tragedies. These, however well acted, never quite came up to what he expected of them from reading; they lost some of their power to excite the imagination that the words evoked when read alone especially by the evening fireside, the best

MRS JORDAN IN THE
CHARACTER OF VIOLA in *Twelfth
Night*: detail from a painting by
John Hoppner

situation, he said, in which to appreciate Shakespeare. He also felt
that though loss of illusion weakened the impact of tragedy, it
positively enhanced that given by comedy. The spectacle of cowar-
dice, for example, painful in real life, became a source of delight when
part of a brilliant comic performance. The playgoer enjoyed it all the
more because he did not quite believe in it, and so could appreciate its
skill in a mood of amused detachment.

For the rest, Lamb found a charm in everything connected with
playgoing; the breathless, crowded climb to the gallery, to be greeted
by bright strong-smelling oil lamps, by the voices of the girl
attendants crying 'Choose a bill of the play, Choose an orange!', by the
scrape of the violins tuning up to introduce the music which preluded
the thrill that never failed to sweep over him at the rise of the curtain.
Before long he met some friends who introduced him back-stage, to
dressing room and Green Room. He enjoyed himself there as much as
he did in the auditorium. Unlike many playgoers, Lamb was not
disappointed by meeting actors off stage. On the contrary, he found

RICHARD SUETT AS DICKY GOSSIP in Hoare's *My Grandmother*, Haymarket
Theatre, 1793: painting by Samuel de Wilde

them an attractive race; he liked their friendliness and vivacity and
lack of inhibition. He was interested also to compare their private with
their professional personalities, to note that Dickie Suett was the same
'wild Robin Goodfellow' behind the scenes as he was on the stage,
whereas Dodd, the inimitable impersonator of foolish Sir Andrew,
was in real life notable for his intelligence and dignity.

Lamb's enthusiasm for literature and the theatre combined to
inspire his first published work. In December 1794 the *Morning
Chronicle* printed a poem by him celebrating the shudders and tears
roused in him by the acting of Mrs. Siddons. This was not his only
poem; it was during these years that the creative impulse first began to
stir in him. The results were not very notable. Lamb's early works
consist mainly of mild little elegiac pieces couched in limp and
conventionally phrased verses recording boyhood joys and moonlit
beautiful evenings and, of course, regret for the love of lost Ann.
Lamb's impulse to express himself had not yet found a mode in which
to convey his live and individual personality. His verses however were
unpretentious and sincere and pleased such friends as he chose to
show them to.

[IV]

Friends meant as much to him as literature did; and he had a growing
number of them. Working long hours, as he did, he met them mainly
at weekends or in the evenings at taverns. They were a mixed lot.
Given that they were friendly and not so strictly decorous as to cramp
his characteristic style, he found himself equally at home with the
elderly and the youthful, the simple and the subtle, the old-fashioned
and the up-to-date. Roughly, his friends divided themselves into two
groups, corresponding to his two prevailing moods; the more
thoughtful and poetic, who foregathered at a tavern called 'The
Salutation and Cat' in Newgate Street, and the more light-hearted
who preferred drinking, perhaps too freely, of Burton Ale at 'The

Feathers' in Hand Court, Holborn, and with whom he could give rein to his delight in nonsense, hoaxes and puns, wild fits of gaiety, and a general enjoyment in making a fool of himself. On the evening of November the fifth, 1794, he appeared at 'The Feathers' in a hat with a wide brim which his companions, a group of old schoolfellows, proceeded to pin up round the crown in a grotesque fashion. Thus attired, Lamb, walking home, was accosted by a group of revellers. 'The veritable guy' they cried, and picking him up they carried him to St. Paul's churchyard where they deposited him on a high post leaving him to get down as best he might. Lamb entered into the joke and amused himself telling the story to his friends, who afterwards often referred to him as 'the veritable guy'. He was never to be one to stand on his dignity. 'I do not want to be respected,' he once said, 'I do not respect myself.' The chief of his light-hearted friends was Thomas White, an old schoolfellow. He was a genial, flamboyant personality, celebrated for his gift of mimicry, who took a special and enthusiastic delight in the personality and conversation of Falstaff as described by Shakespeare, impersonated him at masquerades, and a year or two later published a book of imaginary letters by Falstaff, composed by himself. Lamb helped him with this; he was very fond of White, who combined a fantastic 'Gothic' style of humour with an uncommonly kind heart. It was typical of White to feel so sorry for the ragged, half-starved boy chimney sweeps of London that he instituted an annual feast of sausages and ale for them at Smithfields. With amused affection Lamb watched White presiding over this festivity with dramatic zest, pressing his youthful guests to yet one more succulent morsel of sausage, gaily embracing the fat old women who were cooking them. White was to continue exuberant and kindly all his life, so that when thirty years later he died 'he has carried away half the fun of my world', said Charles Lamb.

In these early years the two saw so much of one another that many people took White to be Lamb's closest friend. In fact he was never intimate with him. Jolly good-hearted White was not the man to enter into Lamb's deeper, more imaginative and poetic side; nor would Lamb have felt able to confide in White about his nervous anxieties. Here he found more understanding at the 'Salutation' tavern in the company of another and more unusual old schoolfellow. Coleridge, who had spent the last few years away at Cambridge and elsewhere, had in 1794 come back to London, where he re-entered Lamb's life to become, next to Mary, the most important figure in his history. This was not surprising. The twenty-two-year-old Coleridge was a personality of compelling fascination. He was also a very strange one. The contrast to be observed in his countenance between noble brow and feeble chin was all too accurate a symbol of the spirit within: such a freakish mixture of incongruous characteristics as to bewilder anyone who came into contact with him. On the one hand he was a man of commanding literary and intellectual genius, the future author of some supreme poetic masterpieces, and an impressive pioneer in ideas about literature, politics and metaphysics; on the other he was a man so lacking in willpower and sense of reality as to be relied on to mismanage alike his private and his professional affairs. Faced with failure in these matters, he would apologise abjectly and proceed to seek comfort in some improbable scheme of reformation; or, in later years, in ever increasing doses of laudanum. Yet neither of them stopped his mind working for long. Throughout his life he continued to analyse and speculate originally and fruitfully. To study Coleridge's history is to be left with impressions in turn awe-inspiring and pathetic, glorious and farcical. These had already shewn themselves by 1794. Coleridge had arrived at Cambridge with a considerable reputation which he confirmed by soon winning a university prize. Success, however, was then followed by collapse. He spent too much, talked too much, and neglected his work, with the result that he was soon landed in an acute financial and psychological crisis. To escape from this he impulsively enlisted in a dragoon regiment under the alias of Silas Tomkyn Comberbach. It proved a distressingly appropriate name. The Dragoons were a cavalry regiment and Trooper Comberbach turned out to be incapable of sitting on the back of a horse for more than a few moments. Indeed in every way Coleridge was unfitted to be a soldier. Within a few months he managed with the help of friends to get out of the army. By the end of the year he was out of Cambridge too, and without having achieved a degree. Now came another turn of the wheel. A free man, he made some new congenial friends, notably Robert Southey, a young man with a big nose and bright eyes, one day to become a respectable Poet Laureate, but at this time a full-blooded romantic rebel. The two found themselves in agreement about many things, in particular about the shocking corruption of the Old World. They even meditated emigrating to America with the idea of founding an ideal and communal society there, to be named Pantisocracy. Stimulated by Southey's company, and also by his own new found sense of liberty, Coleridge's genius now took over, to rise above his weaknesses. By the time he and Lamb had met again it was ablaze with an illuminating brilliance.

There was much for it to illuminate. The last years of the eighteenth century were a dark, chaotic period, the stormy transition from the old to the modern world. The effect of the French Revolution and of the ideas inspiring it was to set many thoughtful persons such as Wordsworth questioning the truth of the established beliefs and institutions – religious, political, aesthetic – of the society of which they had been born. Questioning did not depress them. On the contrary they sought hopefully and enthusiastically to discover new beliefs and institutions which corresponded more with their views of what was ideally right. They were, however, seldom clear what form these new beliefs and institutions should take, and were ready to listen to anyone who had views on the subject. No one had

Opposite: WILLIAM WORDSWORTH, aged twenty-eight: painting by William Shuter, 1798

more views than Coleridge. He had read and thought about such things ever since he was a boy; his mind, further stirred by the exciting events that were then taking place in the world, now seethed with ideas. These ideas often changed – Coleridge found it hard to come to final conclusions – and they were sometimes obscure: but they were always fresh, original and adventurous, while their occasional obscurity only served to add to them the charm of mystery. Further – and this it was that first made him famous amongst his contemporaries – he had an extraordinary gift for imparting his views to others. Coleridge's talks in the cloisters of Christ's Hospital had been rehearsals for even more impressive performances. The list of his great friends include some of the most distinguished names in English literary history – Wordsworth, Hazlitt, de Quincey; and all of them agree that the talk of the young Coleridge was incomparably the most wonderful they had ever known. Certainly it was very unlike most talk, according to their accounts of it. Listen to Hazlitt's:

> His genius at that time had angelic wings, and fed on manna. He talked on for ever; and you wished him to talk on for ever. His thoughts did not seem to come with labour and effort; but as if borne on the gusts of genius, and as if the wings of his imagination lifted him from off his feet. His voice rolled on the ear like the pealing organ, and its sound alone was the music of thought. His mind was clothed with wings; and raised on them, he lifted philosophy to heaven. In his descriptions, you then saw the progress of human happiness and liberty in bright and never-ending succession, like the steps of Jacob's ladder. . .

As may be inferred from this rapturous description, Coleridge's

Opposite: SAMUEL TAYLOR COLERIDGE, aged twenty-three: painting by Peter Vandyke, 1795

talk was the more singular from the fact that it was generally a solo performance, a tireless monologue. This was not immediately apparent. He would wait, polite and benign, till someone made a remark that stirred his interest. Tentatively the soft seductive voice would begin to comment on it, then gradually, as his mind grew absorbed in his theme, his tones would grow more impassioned and his language richer and more heightened, till he was launched on a flight of sustained and spell-binding eloquence, by means of which he carried his hearers with him on a thrilling journey of intellectual exploration, touching now on politics, now on metaphysics, now on literature, its course brightened at every turn by apt vivid phrases, thought-provoking axioms and startling beautiful images, lit up now and again by a gleam of unearthly magic which revealed him as the future author of 'The Ancient Mariner'. When in full flood, these monologues of Coleridge could go on for several hours on end; yet the spellbound listeners never wanted them to stop. This seems all the more surprising in view of the fact that Coleridge was apparently indifferent to the reactions of his audience, for, we are told, if during a rare pause one of his hearers ventured to disagree with anything he said he would listen courteously, even seeming to concede the point made, but would then go on talking as if he had never been interrupted. In spite of this young Wordsworth, young Hazlitt and young De Quincey listened to Coleridge for as long as he was willing to continue.

So did young Lamb; he too compared Coleridge's talk to that of an angel. Not all of it found him responsive. He was impenitently personal and private in his sympathies; even Coleridge could not get Charles Lamb to take an interest in the French Revolution. Or in theological doctrine – though he would listen absorbedly to anything Coleridge had to say about religion as it spoke to the individual soul. But it was their common interest in literature that brought the two together and which they talked about most. Here Coleridge's effect on Lamb was electric. The breadth of his reading, the far-reaching boldness of his thought, lit up by the towering flame of his enthusiasm, revealed the literary scene in a new and majestic perspective, filling Lamb's mind with fresh ideas and firing his enthusiasm to a similar fervour. The two friends read together, wrote poems which they showed to each other and planned to publish in a joint volume. Meanwhile they endlessly discussed literature. It could be called discussion for – and this is the measure of their mental sympathy – in Lamb's company Coleridge's talk became a little less of a monologue. Inevitably he talked the most, he had the most to say. But Lamb had things to say in return. Browsing in Mr. Salt's library and the bookstalls of London, he had read some books which Coleridge had not, and he introduced them to him. Moreover, Lamb's literary insights, more intuitive than those of Coleridge, were equally subtle and original and perceptive. 'A man of uncommon genius,' so Coleridge described Lamb to a friend. The impact of the two minds on each other was extraordinary and fruitful; the two animated youths enjoying talk and egg-nog till late into the night at the 'Salutation' tavern were, although they might not know it, inaugurating a whole new critical approach to literature.

As they got to know each other better they grew more intimate. Their conversations became personal as well as literary. Each confided to the other his secret hopes and fears and joys and anxieties, expatiated on his moments of happiness, his fits of depression; each asked the other's advice about any problem disturbing his emotional life. Coleridge at this period was involved in an acute problem. Just before he came to London he had impulsively engaged himself to marry a Miss Sarah Fricker, only to discover shortly afterwards that he was more in love with a Miss Mary Evans. Agitatedly he consulted Lamb about how he was to get out of this awkward situation. Lamb listened sympathetically, but also with a smile. For all that he admired Coleridge so much, he was too observant not to recognise his weaknesses and to be amused by them. He did not let himself think worse of Coleridge on this account: he was too fond of him. Moreover, his taste for irony led him to find Coleridge's particular weaknesses entertaining. For the rest, he did what he could to help him, spoke comforting words, and, in spite of the fact that he was himself always hard up, sometimes unasked settled an unpaid bill of Coleridge's for him. When it came to personal and practical matters the roles of the two friends were reversed: Lamb became the mature responsible guide whom the vacillating and irresponsible Coleridge looked up to for advice and assistance. Lamb, it should be added, would not have agreed to this view of their relationship. He was always to speak as if Coleridge owed nothing to him, whereas he owed Coleridge everything. Twenty years later he dedicated a volume to him in memory of their old suppers at the 'Salutation' tavern when, as he put it 'Coleridge kindled in him if not the power, yet the love of poetry and beauty and kindliness.' These words show how overwhelming was his feeling of gratitude to Coleridge. More overwhelming than his regard for truth, for Lamb in fact had loved poetry and beauty long before those suppers at the 'Salutation' tavern. As for kindliness, Lamb had always been kindly – and more effectively than ever Coleridge was.

'THE SALUTATION AND CAT' nineteenth-century engraving

CHAPTER IV : TRAGEDY

[1]

Lamb's first surviving letter was written on May 17, 1796. It was addressed to Coleridge; and towards the end of it, after giving Coleridge some news about his friends and making a few comments on his writing, it goes on as follows:

> My life has been somewhat diversified of late. The six weeks that finished last year and began this, your very humble servant spent very agreeably in a mad house at Hoxton – I am got somewhat rational now and don't bite anyone. But mad I was – and many a vagary my imagination played with me.

This statement must have startled Coleridge: it startles the twentieth-century reader: and all the more because time and chance have left us little information about Lamb's state of mind and spirits during the previous two years. A few facts, gleaned from subsequent letters, suggest some explanation. At first, after he had left school, what with books and plays and White's jokes and Coleridge's talk he had been in the main a happy man. But by 1794 shadows began to gather and gradually darken his days. They arose from various quarters. Already his growing realisation that he had lost Ann Simmons had begun to lower his spirits. His home too – moved now from the Temple to Little Queen Street, off Holborn – was not the cheerful place it used to be. His father was growing senile; with mind and memory nearly gone he sat about, querulously demanding that someone should play cards with him. At the same time Mrs. Lamb was suffering from a complaint which partially paralysed her. This meant that Mary, who shared her home and even her bed, passed most of her days and nights nursing her mother. Since she was also trying to increase the family's small income by earning her living as a dressmaker, this put a dangerous strain on her delicate nerves which found vent in ominous irrational outbursts. Finally, Lamb was bereft of the company of Coleridge. In the spring of 1795 Southey, by this time brother-in-law of Coleridge's deserted fiancée, Sarah Fricker, had, at the behest of his wife's family, come up to London and firmly taken the reluctant Coleridge back to Bristol, there to get married and, it was hoped, to settle down. Coleridge was the single friend with whom Lamb felt intimate enough to unbosom himself about his personal troubles; he was also the one man who could stimulate his thoughts and imagination in such a way as to make him forget these troubles, if only for a moment.

Disappointment in love, trouble at home, the absence of Coleridge – the combination of these was enough deeply to disturb the balance on which Lamb's nervous stability rested. This, at twenty-one years of age, and but lately emerged from adolescence, was a precarious balance. On the one hand was his gift for enjoying himself and his fits of wild high spirits; on the other was his propensity to sudden, morbid moods of melancholy, and strange, morbid melancholy imaginings: the sign in him of a streak of hereditary madness. There must always have been a danger that his darker side might get the better of his brighter side. In his early twenties this happened. His troubles began more and more to affect his spirits, his gaiety flagged, and, with it, his sociability. If he could not enjoy himself in other people's company – join in their jokes and make jokes of his own – he shrank from it. When not at his office, he began to withdraw into solitude. Mary, it is true, was always there to help him fight his depression and be devoted and understanding. He loved her for it, if possible more than ever. But this very fact made her a source of pain as well as comfort: for often his depression found vent in explosions of complaint and irritation, which later he thought must have distressed her. This affected him with a sense of guilt which, in its turn, added to his depression.

Anyway, Mary's devotion was of no avail. During 1795 Lamb's nervous condition rapidly deteriorated till in the winter he had a breakdown so bad that he had to be taken off to a private asylum in Hoxton, suffering from delusions. Some of these were surprising. At one moment, for instance, he thought he was young Norval, the hero of *Douglas*, a popular drama of the period, and a robust handsome warrior of noble birth flourishing in the age of the Vikings. This must surely have been a pleasant change from knowing himself to be a worried, poorly paid city clerk with spindly legs and a stammer, living in the reign of George the Third. Indeed Lamb, as he later ruefully acknowledged, was sometimes happier mad than he had ever been when sane. 'At some future time,' he told Coleridge, 'I will amuse you with an account as full as my memory will permit of the strange turn my frenzy took . . while it lasted I had many many hours of pure happiness . . Dream not of having tasted all the grandeur and wildness of Fancy, till you have gone mad.' But he had also experienced hours of crazy anguish and horror.

Acute though his madness seemed to have been, it was brief. By the time he wrote to Coleridge he had been sane for nearly six months. But he had not yet got his spirits back. Understandably, the prospect before him remained dreary. His father was still senile, his mother still an invalid, Coleridge still away: so that all too often he was still oppressed by feelings of loneliness yet at the same time shrinking instinctively from the company of his fellows. He wrote to Coleridge on June 10:

> Thank you for your frequent letters; you are the only correspondent and I might add the only friend I have in the world. I go nowhere and have no acquaintance. Slow of speech and reserved of manners, no one seeks or cares for my society and I am left alone . . When I read in your little volume, your 19th Effusion, or the 28th or 29th or what you call the 'Sigh' I think I hear *you* again. I imagine to myself the little smoky room at the Salutation and Cat, where we have sat together thro' the winter nights, beguiling the cares of life with Poesy. When you left

LINCOLN'S INN FIELDS, as seen from Great Queen Street: aquatint in J.B. Papworth's *Select Views of London*, 1816. At the time of Charles Lamb's nervous breakdown and Mary's attack on her mother the Lambs were living at 7, Little

Queen Street, which used to run from High Holborn down to Great Queen Street, and is now absorbed into the top end of Kingsway. The house would have been a few yards to the left of the point at which the drawing for this aquatint was made.

London I felt a dismal void in my heart. I found myself cut off at one and the same time from two most dear to me. 'How blest with Ye the Path could I have trod of Quiet Life.' . . . In your conversation you had blended so many pleasant fancies, that they cheated me of my grief. But in your absence, the tide of melancholy rushed in again, and did its worst Mischief by overwhelming my Reason. I have recovered. But feel a stupor that makes me indifferent to the hopes and fears of this life. I sometimes wish to introduce a religious turn of mind, but habits are strong things, and my religious fervors are confined alas to some fleeting moments of occasional solitary devotion. . . .

And again, a few days later:

I have been drinking egg-hot and smoking Oronooko (associated circumstances which ever forcibly recall to my mind our evenings and nights at the Salutation); my eyes and brain are heavy and asleep, but my heart is awake; and if words came as ready as ideas, and ideas as feelings, I could say ten hundred kind things. Coleridge, you know not my supreme happiness at having one on earth (though counties separate us) whom I can call a friend. . . . I am writing at random and half tipsy, which you may not equally understand, as you will be sober when you read it; but my sober and my half-tipsy hours you are alike a sharer-in. Goodnight.

From these quotations we learn something of the ways in which Lamb sought to deal with his depression. The first, suggested by Coleridge, was by spiritual means, prayer and meditation. Lamb tried these but without great success. As will appear more fully later, he was not made to be a devotee. The second quotation indicates that he tried to cheer himself up by material means. At once high-strung and convivial, Lamb readily responded to the effects of alcohol. On happy evenings at the 'Feathers' he used to drink for enjoyment: now, when depressed, he turned to drink for comfort. Since he had a weak head this meant that now and again he was, to use his own phrase, 'half-tipsy'.

Half-tipsiness for a man with a weak head was not a condition to do him much harm; it never seems to have hindered him from doing his work. Nor did it now delay his recovery from his breakdown; for, in spite of his prevailing mood of melancholy, he was on the way to recovery. His emotional outbursts took up a smaller and smaller part of his letters to Coleridge. The rest was filled with talk about literature and his friends, expressed in a relaxed and humorous tone. He continued in the same tone even when referring to his madness. Indeed there is something disconcerting and even comic in the casual way in which he breaks the news to Coleridge that he had just been spending months as a patient in a lunatic asylum, as if this was a minor and commonplace misfortune that might happen to anyone, and which therefore he should not make a fuss about. As a matter of fact, and, although he cannot have known it, he had some reason to be cheerful, for his recovery was to be permanent. Never again – even when faced with far worse troubles – did he show any sign of such another breakdown. It was as if experience of madness and recovery had, between them, matured him, so that his restored nervous balance now rested on a new and firm foundation of self-knowledge and self-control. He had learned that the forces in him making for sanity were stronger than those making for madness; and, instinctively, he now knew how to summon them to his help when needed.

Meanwhile he was content to live in the present, taking things as they came with a sort of playful stoicism. Trouble he accepted as an inevitable feature of man's lot, but he hoped that, with luck and with some fun thrown in, his own lot might not prove unduly painful.

[11]

Very soon, however, an event took place so dreadful as to render any such hope vain. There appeared in the *Whitehall Evening Post* on

Monday September 26, 1796, the following item of news:-

On Friday afternoon the Coroner and a respectable Jury sat on the body of a Lady in the neighbourhood of Holborn, who died in consequence of a wound from her daughter the preceding day. It appeared by the evidence adduced, that while the family were preparing for dinner, the young lady seized a case knife laying on the table, and in a menacing manner pursued a little girl, her apprentice, round the room; on the eager calls of her helpless infirm mother to forbear, she renounced the first object, and with loud shrieks approached her parent. The child by her cries quickly brought up the landlord of the house, but too late – the dreadful scene presented to him the mother lifeless, pierced to the heart, on a chair, her daughter yet wildly standing over her with the fatal knife, and the venerable old man, her father, weeping by her side, himself bleeding at the forehead from the effects of a severe blow he received from one of the forks she had been madly hurling about the room.

For a few days prior to this the family had observed some symptoms of insanity in her, which had so much increased on the Wednesday evening, that her brother, early the next morning went in quest of Dr. Pitcairn – had that gentleman been met with, the fatal catastrophe had, in all probability, been prevented.

It seems the young Lady had been once before, in her earlier years, deranged, from the harassing fatigues of too much business. As her carriage towards her mother was ever affectionate in the extreme, it is believed that to the increased attentiveness, which her parents infirmities called for by day and night, is to be attributed the present insanity of this ill-fated young woman . . . The jury of course brought in their Verdict, Lunacy. The above unfortunate young person is a Miss Lamb, a mantua-maker in Little Queen Street, Lincoln's-inn-Fields. She has been since removed to Islington mad-house.

This account does not mention that Charles – for he was the brother who had gone the day before to look for a doctor – was also present at the scene of death and that it was he who managed to get the knife away from his sister before she had done any more harm with it. Indeed, from that moment he took command of the situation. He had to; there was no-one else. His father was in his dotage; old Aunt Hetty had collapsed, overcome by the horrors which she had witnessed; his brother John, while professing sympathy, shrank back, determined to be as little involved as possible in so painful an affair. Charles it was, therefore, who had to take responsibility for the Lamb family and its future. He made arrangements for the funeral and for the gathering of friends afterwards which, even in these grim circumstances, was considered a necessary part of the ritual; it was he who saw to it that his father and aunt were looked after now Mary had gone. He also paid regular visits to the private asylum where she was confined in order to see that she was being properly treated.

All these things the stammering twenty-one-year-old Charles managed to do with efficiency and apparent calm. After the first few days, things got a little easier. Friends came in to help, notably his old school friend, Sam Le Grice, who, finding that old Mr. Lamb (apparently forgetful of what had passed) was fretfully demanding entertainment, came everyday to play cribbage with him for hours on end. Aunt Hetty, too, was taken off Charles's hands by an elderly and well-off female relative, who offered to have her to live with her, in order to make life easier for her hard-working nephew and senile brother. Best of all, after ten days or so, Mary came to her senses. Her recovery was accompanied by a strange spiritual experience. At the same time that she learned what she had done in her madness, she felt her spirit flooded with a sense of serenity born of the conviction that God himself wished her to know that she was in no way to blame for the terrible act she had committed but should look on it as an affliction visited on her by the Divine Will for some mysterious purpose; and that the soul of her dead mother was aware of this. In a note to Charles

Mary wrote:

> I have no bad terrifying dreams. At midnight when I happen to
> awake, the nurse sleeping by the side of me, with the noise of the
> poor mad people around me, I have no fear. The spirit of my
> mother seems to descend and smile upon me and bid me live to
> enjoy the life and reason which the Almightly has given me – I
> shall see her again in heaven; she will then understand me better.

This passage suggests that, just because Mary did love her mother
very much, she was proportionately wounded by what seemed to her a
rejection of that love. Rejected love turned at times to something like
hate; a hate which, in her madness and when apparently thwarted by
her mother, burst out in violence. This suggestion is encouraged by
the fact that Mary's recovery was accompanied by a visionary sense
that her mother, now translated into a better world, loved her as she
had never done in life. Charles was deeply moved by the words in
Mary's letter. He commented:

> Poor Mary, my mother indeed never understood her right. She
> loved us all with a mother's love; but in opinion, in feeling and
> sentiment and disposition, bore so distant resemblance to her
> daughter that she never understood her right – never could
> believe how much she loved her – but met her caresses, her
> protestation of filial affection too frequently with coldness and
> repulse.

Charles had long resented this on Mary's behalf; and especially in
view of the fact that his mother so obviously preferred the handsome
but unworthy John. Yet he also felt remorse for his resentment, for he
realised that to him his mother had been a good and affectionate
parent. He recalled happy days as a child playing with her, and
blamed himself that when older he had sometimes felt irritated with

her, and had shown it. These mixed feelings he poured out to Coleridge. Whenever he had a spare moment he turned to scribble a letter to him as to the one living being to whom he could open his anguished heart. A few days after the disaster he wrote:

> My dearest friend, White or some of my friends or the public papers by this time may have informed you of the terrible calamities that have fallen on our family . . . God has preserved to me my senses – I eat and drink and sleep, and have my judgment I believe very sound. My poor father was slightly wounded, and I am left to take care of him and my aunt . . . thank God I am very calm and composed, and able to do the best that remains to do. Write – as religious a letter as possible – but no mention of what is gone and done with – with me the former things are passed away, and I have something more to do than to feel – God almighty have us all in his keeping . . mention nothing of poetry. I have destroyed every vestige of past vanities of that kind.

Coleridge's reply showed affectionate conern; also a characteristic tendency to see the events as part of the sublime drama of human destiny as conceived of by his energetic imagination:

> Your letter, my friend, struck me with a mighty horror. It rushed upon me and stupefied my feelings. You bid me to write you a religious letter; I am not a man who would attempt to insult the greatness of your anguish by another consolation. Heaven knows that in the easiest fortunes there is much dissatisfaction and weariness of spirit; much that calls for the exercise of patience and resignation; but in storms, like these, that shake the dwelling and make the heart tremble, there is no middle way between despair and the yielding up of the whole spirit unto the guidance of faith. And surely it is a matter of joy, that your faith in Jesus has been preserved; the Comforter that should relieve you is not far from

you . . . Your poor father is, I hope, almost senseless of the calamity; the unconscious instrument of Divine Providence knows it not, and your mother is in heaven. It is sweet to be roused from a frightful dream by the song of birds, and the gladsome rays of the morning. Ah, how infinitely more sweet to be awakened from the blackness and amazement of a sudden horror by the glories of God manifest, and the hallelujahs of angels. As to what regards yourself, I approve altogether of your abandoning what you justly call vanities. I look upon you as a man, called by sorrow and anguish and a strange desolation of hopes into quietness, and a soul set apart and made peculiar to God . . .

In the event, Lamb got no further than burning a few poems. His resolution had been an unconsidered expression of an emotional impulse prompted immediately after his mother's death by a sense that the appalling tragedy in which he had been involved had cut him off for ever from his past and its pleasures; especially such deluding pleasures as writing poetry. To signify this, and as a gesture of expiation, he swore to write no more. Impulse and gesture were both irrational, a sign of a momentary lack of balance. Before long Lamb recognised this; by October he was writing poetry again.

His resolution to stop doing so was the only irrational sign that he showed during the whole terrible crisis. Otherwise his spirit was as collected as his demeanour suggested. He explained to Coleridge:

Wonderful as it is to tell, I have never once been otherwise than collected, and calm; even on the dreadful day and in the midst of the terrible scene I preserved a tranquillity, which bystanders may have construed into indifference, a tranquillity not of despair; is it folly or sin in me to say that it was a religious principle that most supported me? I allow much to other favourable circumst-ances. I felt that I had something else to do than to regret; on that first evening my Aunt was lying insensible, to all appearance like one dying – my father, with his poor forehead plaistered over from a wound he had received from a daughter dearly loved by him, and who loved him no less dearly – my mother a dead and murder'd corpse in the next room – yet was I wonderfully supported. I closed not my eyes in sleep that night, but lay without terrors and without despair. I have lost no sleep since. I had been long used not to rest in things of sense, had endeavoured after a comprehension of mind, unsatisfied with the 'ignorant present time,' and this kept me up . . . One little incident may serve to make you understand my way of managing my mind. Within a day or two after the fatal one, we drest for dinner a tongue which we had salted for some weeks in the house. As I sat down a feeling like remorse struck me, – this tongue poor Mary got for me, and can I partake of it now, when she is far away? – a thought occurred and relieved me, – if I give in to this way of feeling, there is not a chair, a room, an object in our rooms, that will not awaken the keenest griefs, I must rise above such weaknesses. – I hope this was not want of true feeling. I did not let this carry me, tho', too far. On the very 2d day (I date from the day of horrors) as is usual in such cases there were a matter of 20 people, I do think, supping in our room. They prevailed on me to eat with them (for to eat I never refused). They were all making merry in the room, – some had come from friendship, some from busy curiosity, and some from interest; I was going to partake with them, when my recollection came that my poor dead mother was lying in the next room, the very next room, a mother who thro' life wished nothing but her children's welfare – indignation, the rage of grief, something like remorse, rushed upon my mind in an agony of emotion, – I found my way mechanically to the adjoining room, and fell on my knees by the side of her coffin, asking forgiveness of heaven, and sometimes of her, for forgetting her so soon. Tranquillity returned, and it was the only violent emotion that mastered me, and I think it did me good.

It seems surprising that he could keep calm considering that his own nervous system was delicate and that less than a year before he had himself spent several months as a patient in a lunatic asylum. In fact, his experience of madness had inoculated him against another such breakdown: he had learned that it was possible to suffer extreme anguish of spirit and yet recover from it. This enabled him to see his situation in a larger more hopeful perspective, and so to survey it with composure. All the same, he could not have risen to the occasion as he did had he not been impelled by another and personal motive. Unbidden and irresistible, his love for Mary rose up to possess him completely so that he forgot any concern for himself in his concern for her. His brother, John, more human than heroic, feared that Charles was setting him an unwelcome example of extreme unselfishness and cautioned him against it. It was not reasonable, he said, that Charles should sacrifice legitimate interests and pleasures in order to give extra care to a crazy sister. Charles listened to his words unmoved. In his eyes it was John, not himself, who was unreasonable. 'I fear for his mind,' he said; he feared for the mind of anyone who could not recognise that Mary's goodness and sweetness were such that every other consideration ought to give way to helping her in her horrible misfortune. To help Mary became the single object to which Charles's whole being became committed; so much so, that he found he could carry on living with an appearance, even a feeling, of calm.

Calm enough to be objective – this showed itself in his attitude to Coleridge. Though Charles continued to find him a chief source of spiritual comfort, he did not always agree with his particular counsels. He could not accept, for instance, Coleridge's suggestion that he should look on his troubles as a means by which he could share in the Divine sufferings of Christ. Apart from the fact that, as a Unitarian, he did not believe Christ was Divine in the sense implied by Coleridge's words, he thought that for a man to try and identify with God in such a way was inconsistent with the beautiful simplicity of the Christian Gospel.

Now and again, too, he began to see Coleridge as in some ways comical. With the progress of Mary's recovery, calm brightened occasionally to cheerfulness: and a cheerfulness that, as always with Charles Lamb, glinted with amusement. It appeared from Coleridge's letters that his active, as contrasted with his mental life, continued to be a laughable confusion of dreamy hopes and unpractical plans and congenital indecision. One day he is proposing to be a journalist, the next to take a job as a tutor, the third to set up as a hermit devoting himself to poetry and gardening in a cottage at Nether Stowey in Somerset. He wrote announcing these successive projects to Lamb, who could not repress a smile. He wrote:

> You seem to be taking up splendid schemes of fortune only to lay them down again; and your fortunes are an *ignis fatuus* that has been conducting you in thought from Lancaster Court, Strand, to somewhere near Matlock; then jumping across to Doctor Somebody's, whose sons' tutor you are likely to be; and would to God that the dancing demon may take you, at last in peace and comfort, to the life and labours of a cottager.

He added apologetically:

> You see from the above awkward playfulness of fancy that my spirits are not quite depressed; I should ill deserve God's blessings which, since the late terrible event, have come down in mercy upon us, if I indulged regret or querulousness. Mary continues serene and cheerful.

She did not continue serene long: in December she was mad again. Now that she was under professional care, it was possible to give her treatment that kept her madness relatively under control. But mad she was; and in order to be near enough to her to keep a close watch over her condition Charles decided that he and his father must move

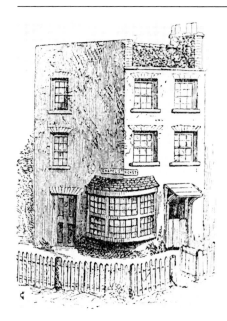

15 CHAPEL STREET, PENTONVILLE: nineteenth-century engraving. This was the house at the corner of High Street, Pentonville, to which Lamb moved with his father and Aunt Hetty at the end of 1796. It was not far from the Islington madhouse where Mary Lamb was living. Lamb moved to No. 36 in the same street in 1799, after his father's death, and Mary joined him there. They left Pentonville a year later and went to live in Southampton Buildings, Chancery Lane.

house again, this time from Little Queen Street to 45 Chapel Street, Pentonville. Things were not made easier for Charles that winter by old Mr. Lamb, who was increasingly senile; 'If you won't play cribbage with me,' he would complain to his son, arriving tired from a long day's work at the East India Office, 'you might as well not come home at all!' Also he had Aunt Hetty on his hands again. Very soon her rich relation had found her company so trying – 'indolent and mulish' was how she described her – that she returned her to the Lambs, explaining, not very convincingly, that she knew they loved their aunt so much that they must be missing her. Charles now found himself, at a time when he could ill afford it, faced with the trouble and expense of having yet another semi-senile relative to look after. Luckily it was not for long. Aunt Hetty died in February. Amused, affectionate memories of her in his early days crowded into Charles's mind and touched his heart. Yet he had to admit that her death was a relief.

With the new year his youthful and resilient spirits began to rise. 'I recognise feelings which I may taste again, if tranquillity has not taken her flight for ever; I will believe that I shall be happy, very happy again,' he wrote to Coleridge; and his letters to him, though still partly about his spiritual state, were more and more concerned with literary subjects, especially Coleridge's poems and his own. He also began to cultivate other friendships, notably with Southey. Thus, first one and then another gleam of sunshine started to pierce the clouds that had long overcast his days.

In the Spring an event occurred that raised hopes of dispersing them altogether. Mary had for some time shewn signs of getting better. By the beginning of April she appeared to have recovered. Was it possible, Charles wondered, that she was going to remain so? If so, he would be granted what had come to be his heart's desire. Meanwhile what was to be done with her? Charles naturally wanted her to resume her old way of life, with the dreadful past completely forgotten. But in view of her history the Medical Authorities were nervous about allowing her to be at large, and with the possibility of another relapse, unless someone was prepared to take full respons- ibility for her. Otherwise she had better be confined for life to a Public Asylum. Charles did not hesitate: in spite of the urgings of his brother John who thought it would be a comfort to her family to have her safely put away in the Asylum, he came forward and solemnly promised to take complete and life-long responsibility for her. For the time being he could not have her to live with him at home; the sight of her, it was thought, would upset his old father too much. But he found lodgings for her kept by people he could trust to treat her kindly and close enough to where he lived for him to be able to spend a great part of his free time in her company.

His decision was the most important act of his life, and determined the whole of its subsequent course. It committed him almost certainly to stay permanently at the East India Office; for his job there was safe and ensured that he would be able to support Mary as well as himself and his father. Almost equally certainly, it committed him to remaining all his life a bachelor. Apart from the fact that he was unlikely to find a wife willing to marry a man with a potentially crazy sister permanently under his care, the salary he earned was hardly enough to support three persons. By making this promise, Charles Lamb was, at the age of twenty-two, condemning himself to what was probably going to be a lifetime of hard, ill-paid drudgery, at work he did not care for, without the comfort of a wife, and lived under the shadow of continual anxiety. Yet he never seems to have regarded it as an act of self-sacrifice, let alone claimed any special credit for it. As he saw things, it was the one way he could help Mary. So what else could he do?

[III]

Charles never showed any sign of repenting his decision. But the appalling strain he had gone through left him for the next years deeply disturbed and quite unable to preserve that sense of calm which had risen up so mysteriously in him to carry him through the days of acute crisis. As in early days, he turned for advice to Coleridge, who once again urged him, by means of prayer and meditation, to seek help from God. As in early years, Charles tried to follow this advice and failed. Was this, he asked himself, because he lived among irreligious people and with no-one to give him spiritual sympathy? In search of pious companions, and because he had liked some Quaker writings, he therefore went to a Quaker meeting, but only to find himself forced to listen to a fanatic preacher who, claiming to be under Divine influence, shook and trembled and noisily raved. Charles, so far from feeling edified, found it difficult to prevent himself from laughing. Reading religious books proved no more inspiring. Altogether, his efforts to be more actively devout had not proved successful.

However, as long as Mary was better, he continued to feel better himself. His interest in literature vigorously revived. He read and also wrote a great deal; poems and a short novel called *Rosamund Gray*, which appeared in 1798, his first published volume. The poems were

mostly elegiac little pieces written in gentle blank verse about his
mother and grandmother and other figures from his past, and much
like his earlier poems on similar subjects. The events of the last years
did occasionally alter their tone; from time to time the peaceful flow of
the verses is broken into by cries of remorseful lamentation for
neglecting his mother when she was alive and for failing to meet his
present sorrows more resignedly. Charles Lamb gave vent to his
emotions more frankly and freely in poems which he wrote to relieve
his own feelings than in letters which he wrote knowing that they
would be read by a correspondent.

As literature these poems are not distinguished; nor is *Rosamund
Gray*. Its characters are dim shadows and its story a heterogeneous
muddle: for two thirds of its length a gentle rural idyll, it turns in its
later pages abruptly and unconvincingly into a lurid melodrama in the
manner of the fashionable 'Gothic' romances of the day, now only
remembered as having inspired some entertaining parodies by the
child Jane Austen. Yet fleeting gleams of Lamb's genius do show
themselves in *Rosamund Gray*; in the delicate sense of language
apparent in the writing, and in the fresh country sentiment recalling
his own childhood days at Mackery End that breathes from its early
scenes.

As his literary interests grew stronger, so also did the part played in
his life by his friends, in particular by old friends like Coleridge and
Southey, and by a new friend, Charles Lloyd. Lloyd had entered
Lamb's life in the early months of 1797: a tall, lanky, clumsy youth,
with a manner at once diffident and enthusiastic, who had arrived at
his house bearing an introduction from Coleridge and a bundle of
poems of his own which Coleridge had asked him to show to Lamb.
He was the son of a prosperous Quaker banking family of Bristol
noted for its high-minded and liberal ideals. Himself dreamy and
unpractical, he had, on reaching maturity, reacted enough against his
upbringing to reject Quakerism and banking in favour of a life
dedicated to poetry and philosophising; but he remained high-

minded enough to feel in need of a faith to justify his chosen mode of existence morally. Meeting Coleridge and swept away by his eloquence, he fancied he had found the guide to such a faith. Coleridge, gratified by Lloyd's admiration, flung himself impulsively into friendship with him, read his poems, thought well of them and sent him off to Lamb with a message introducing him as a budding genius. Lamb took to him in his turn and with a warmth that quickly grew to affection: within a few weeks Lloyd had become a loved friend. This was understandable. Here was a responsive, likeable young man offering the possibility of a new and stimulating friendship at a time when his own spirit, oppressed by many months of suffering, was peculiarly ready to welcome one. Mistakenly, as it turned out: Charles Lloyd was not the right friend for Charles Lamb at this moment of his life. He needed to be refreshed and strengthened by the company of someone with good sense and good spirits. Charles Lloyd's Romantic enthusiasm went along with a Romantic nervous instability showing itself in occasional fits of acute melancholy in which he thought that other people, including his closest friends, were against him. In later life these fits were to become a permanent condition. Once again it was Lamb's bad luck to find himself involved in a close relationship with a potential lunatic. As early as the Spring of 1797 Lloyd had to be shut up for some weeks in a mental home, whence he wrote to Lamb explaining that he did not dare open any letters from him for fear of the reproofs he expected to find in them. 'Surely an exquisiteness of feeling that borders on derangement!' remarked Lamb to Coleridge. 'But' he continued, 'I love him more and more': experience had made him think that he ought to be tolerant and even sympathetic to persons suffering from 'derangement'. When Lloyd recovered, the two were soon happily collaborating with Coleridge to produce a volume of poems by the three of them.

In the same summer Coleridge had helped Lamb to make a more fruitful friendship. Himself, during the last two years on one of his

restless peregrinations in the south of England, he had met and made
friends with William Wordsworth. It was to prove the most
momentous event in the lives of both; for the impact of these two men
of genius on each other, at this youthful and seminal period of their
existence, was to kindle the creative flame in each to its highest
intensity of heat and light. It resulted, within two years, in the
publication of the first volume of *Lyrical Ballads*, which, besides
marking the inauguration of a whole new movement in English letters,
was to contain some of the most beautiful poems ever written by
anybody.

Now, in the July of 1797, Coleridge and his family were
temporarily settled in a cottage at the village of Nether Stowey in the
Quantocks with Wordsworth and his sister Dorothy staying near him
at the neighbouring village of Alfoxden. Coleridge, who enjoyed
bringing his friends together and who also wanted to cheer Lamb up,
persuaded him to come down for a week's holiday. Once there, he
spent his days walking with Wordsworth – Coleridge, with what
seems a characteristic mixture of ill-luck and incompetence, had
rendered himself immobile by upsetting some hot milk on his foot – in
the picturesque Somerset countryside, and his evenings either in the
twilit cottage garden or in the little candle-lit cottage livingroom,
listening to Coleridge and Wordsworth reading their poems and
giving their views on life and literature; Coleridge rhapsodising in his
most stirring manner but, out of respect for Wordsworth, for once not
monopolising the conversation. Gaunt, horse-faced Wordsworth,
incapable of Coleridge's eloquence, was yet impressive by reason of
the force of personality evident in his intent visionary gaze and in the
brief pregnant sentences which he uttered slowly in a burring north
country accent. Between them sat Dorothy looking from one to the
other with wild, dark-eyed ardent attention. The contrast made by
their talk to the kind of conversation Lamb had been used to during
the last year made him feel awed and inadequate: after he left he wrote
apologising to Coleridge for a silence which he feared might have

ALFOXDEN PARK: drawn by Miss Sweeting, lithograph by R. and A. Pocock, c. 1840. The Wordsworths were living in Alfoxden when Lamb visited Coleridge at Nether Stowey and they walked over the hills together.

appeared sullen. As a matter of fact this was not the impression he had made on his companions. His charm had been felt by the Wordsworths; he left Nether Stowey their life-long friend. Moreover his occasional contributions to discussion, even if uttered in short and stuttering sentences, had given Wordsworth a deep respect for Lamb's literary judgement, so that for the rest of his life Lamb was one of the few persons whose opinion on his writings Wordsworth sought and valued. As for Coleridge, he referred enthusiastically to the visit in a poem he wrote afterwards about his guests and their country walks:

> Now, my friends emerge
> Beneath the wide wide Heaven – and view again
> The many-steepled tract magnificent

Of hilly fields and meadows, and the sea,
With some fair bark, perhaps, whose sails light up
The slip of smooth clear blue betwixt two Isles
Of purple shadow! Yes! they wander on
In gladness all; but thou, methinks, most glad,
My gentle-hearted Charles! for thou has pined
And hunger'd after Nature, many a year,
In the great City pent, winning thy way
With sad yet patient soul, through evil and pain
And strange calamity! Ah! slowly sink
Behind the western ridge, thou glorious Sun!
Shine in the slant beams of the sinking orb,
Ye purple heath-flowers! richlier burn, ye clouds!
Live in the yellow light, ye distant groves!
And kindle, thou blue Ocean! So my friend
Struck with deep joy may stand, as I have stood,
Silent with swimming sense; yea, gazing round
On the wide landscape, gaze till all doth seem
Less gross than bodily; and of such hues
As veil the Almighty Spirit, when yet he makes
Spirits perceive his presence.

These lines exemplify both Coleridge's genius and his limitations. In
them, the grandeur alike of his poetic vision and of the words in which
he expressed it is not more startling than his blindness to the character
of his friends, even those he had known longest. What could have led
him to think that Charles had ever 'pined' after Nature, or
looked to her to inspire him with a sense of mystical joy. In fact
Lamb's holiday, though pleasant enough, had not succeeded in
dissipating the shadow which his home troubles had cast over his
spirit. Settled back in London, after another short visit to Southey,
and faced with the prospect of a winter of grinding office work or at
home alone with a half-imbecile father, he found this shadow

deepening to a steady, grey depression in which it seemed to him that he was losing his capacity for feeling. The anniversary of his mother's death passed without reviving in him any of the emotions he had felt at the time, neither grief nor horror, nor the sense of exaltation that had risen so strangely to carry him through the days of crisis. All these had vanished, to be replaced by a dull empty gloom. One emotion indeed had not left him; he could still feel anxiety about Mary.

This anxiety was growing; for by the autumn it was clear she was getting worse again. She was so bad by Christmas that Charles had to take her once more to a mental home. With the New Year her condition showed signs of improving. But her relapse had made Charles realise that he must face the fact that her madness might turn out to be recurrent. In consequence his dull depression returned to smother his spirit like a blanket. He was not comforted by Charles Lloyd, who now, recovered from his Spring melancholy and for once in high spirits, used to call on Lamb and tell him he ought not to give way to solitary broodings; rather should he make an effort to cheer himself up by cultivating a more active social life. Lamb, who felt wholly unequal to anything of the kind, was irritated and showed it. Lloyd was hurt: to Lamb's depression was now added a feeling of guilt for having pained one who had only been trying to be kind. One day, therefore, he did attend a party in Lloyd's rooms. Suddenly, as he sat listening to Lloyd playing the piano surrounded by a group of friends, he was seized with an agonised feeling of spiritual loneliness. Unable to bear it, he rushed from the room and thence through the streets of London to the Courts of the Temple. There, stirred by a thousand bitter-sweet memories of past happiness now for ever vanished, his emotions flowed out to well over in some irregular passionate verses, unlike anything else he ever wrote, in which he lamented that all those whom he had loved most were now lost to him: his mother, Ann, Lloyd, Coleridge and, of course, the ever-present, ever-absent Mary.

I had a mother, but she died, and left me
Died prematurely in a day of horrors –
All are gone, the old familiar faces.

I have had playmates, I have had companions,
In my days of childhood, in my youthful school-days –
All, all are gone, the old familiar faces.

I have been laughing, I have been carousing,
Drinking late, sitting late, with my bosom cronies –
All, all are gone, the old familiar faces.

I loved a love once, fairest among women.
Closed are her doors on me, I must not see her –
All, all are gone, the old familiar faces.

I have a friend, a kinder friend has no man.
Like an ingrate, I left my friend abruptly;
Left him, to muse on the old familiar faces.

Ghost-like I paced round the haunts of my childhood.
Earth seemed a desert I was bound to traverse,
Peeking to find the old familiar faces.

Friend of my bosom, thou more than a brother!
Why were thou not born in my father's dwelling?
So might we talk of the old familiar faces.

For some they have died, and some they have left me,
And some are taken from me; all are departed
All, all are gone, the old familiar faces.

MIDDLE TEMPLE HALL: sepia aquatint by Samuel Ireland, in *Picturesque Views of the Inns of Court*, 1800. It was among these long-familiar buildings that Charles Lamb composed the lines quoted on the foregoing page.

[IV]

In fact, a momentary feeling of desolation had led him to exaggerate a little. Though Lloyd was temporarily estranged from him, and Coleridge living too far away for them often to meet, neither was irretrievably lost to Lamb in the sense that his mother was. Yet it was true that his relationship with both one and the other was not what it had been. Within a few months they were actually quarrelling. The story of the quarrel is obscure; our information about it is fragmentary and confusing. What does emerge is that none of the three behaved sensibly. This was unlike Lamb, and is evidence of the nervous strain under which he was suffering. Coleridge and Lloyd, on the other hand, had never been distinguished by good sense; Lloyd was liable to fits of paranoia and Coleridge was the creature of every shifting impulse. It was he who began the trouble. Absorbed perhaps in his friendship with the Wordsworths, he gave Lamb and Lloyd the impression that he had lost interest in them: he neither wrote to them nor answered their letters. Both felt deserted. Indeed Lloyd jumped to the conclusion that Coleridge, for some dark reason of his own, had become his active enemy. Feelings hardened when in November the two came across, in a monthly magazine, some heavy-handed comic verses written by Coleridge under the pen name of Nehemiah Higginbotham which, rightly or not, they took to be parodies of their own serious poems. It was Lloyd who now took to the offensive. Out to take vengeance on his imagined enemy, he brought out a novel called *Edward Oliver* in which, in a fashion hardly disguised, he told the story of Coleridge's undignified army career as Trooper Silas Comberbach. He also tried to get Lamb on his side by repeating to him some hostile remarks alleged to have been made about him by Coleridge. Lamb – and this showed how strained his nerves were – was so provoked as to ask Dorothy Wordsworth to tell Coleridge that he wanted to break off all communications with him. This provoked from Coleridge a letter of self-justification that comically exhibits the less impressive strains in his extraordinary character.

> Lloyd has informed me through Miss Wordsworth that you intend no longer to correspond with me. This has given me little pain; not that I do not love and esteem you, but on the contrary because I am confident that your intentions are pure. You are performing what you deem a duty, and humanly speaking have that merit which can be derived from the performance of a painful duty. Painful, for you would not without struggles abandon me on behalf of a man (Lloyd) who, wholly ignorant of all but your name, became attached to you in consequence of my attachment, caught his from my enthusiasm, and learned to love you at my fireside, when often, while I have been sitting and talking of your sorrows and afflictions, I have stopped my conversations and lifted up wet eyes and prayed for you.

He went on to say that if Lamb and Lloyd were disappointed in him it was their fault for insisting on idealizing him. True possibly of Lloyd, this was notably untrue of Lamb who, throughout their many years of friendship, had recognised Coleridge's weaknesses, though with affectionate amusement. For him, they had always been far outweighed by his wonderful qualities of heart and of head. Lamb was enough recovered to remember these and to want to make things up. He still felt nettled enough to write Coleridge a facetious letter making fun of his habit of seeking to justify his errors on lofty spiritual grounds; but the light-hearted tone of this communication shows that he was no longer seriously annoyed. In the autumn of 1798 Coleridge, fancying that truth might be found in German metaphysics, left for a stay in Westphalia. By the time he departed, he and Lamb were reconciled.

Lamb was the readier for reconciliation because he now realised it was Lloyd more than Coleridge who was to blame for the breach – Lloyd who in a fit of resentment had plotted to make mischief between them. The effect of this discovery was that the intense affection which he had felt for him began to fade. Though Lamb still spoke of him as a friend, from this time on the agitated figure of Charles Lloyd retreats into the background of this story. Not so that of Coleridge. When, a year and a half later, he came back to England, his friendship with Lamb was resumed, to last for the rest of their lives. But it was no longer to be an active creative relationship. The period of mutual cross-fertilisation was over: for the future their geniuses diverged, each to develop on its own very different lines. Nor was Charles Lamb any more to turn to Coleridge for advice as to what to think and how to live.

Meanwhile in the Spring of 1799 old Mr. Lamb died. At last Mary was able to come back and make her home with Charles.

PART TWO

CHARLES LAMB in the dress of a Venetian Senator:
painting by William Hazlitt, 1804

CHAPTER I : PRIME OF LIFE

The year 1799 may stand as the centre and dividing line in Lamb's life story. The years before had been formative and preparatory. From now on his personality appears matured into its final and characteristic form. Since it was in this form that it was to figure in English literary history, his biographer may be allowed to pause for a moment to take a look at him and his way of living, as they were to display themselves during the next twenty-five years or so. It was not a settled way of living, for it was liable to be broken into at any time by one of Mary's attacks of madness. These attacks happened almost every year. When one shewed a clear sign of coming on Charles took her to a private mental home where she stayed – it might be anything from a few weeks to two months – till she recovered. Even the threat of such an attack altered her manner of life. Charles, always on the look-out to note if Mary became over-excited – this was an ominous symptom in a woman who was ordinarily placid – immediately saw that she was kept absolutely quiet: no visitors, no excursions. If her symptoms got worse, resignedly the two made their preparations. Carefully and neatly Mary packed what things she needed, including a strait waistcoat which she accepted she would have to be put into if she showed signs of growing violent. Then together they would walk off to the mental home. Charles Lloyd caught sight of them on one of these melancholy journeys, a pathetic little pair, trudging patiently along and both in tears. Afterwards Charles Lamb would return to a lonely life till Mary was well enough for him to fetch her home again.

It was never to be a permanent home. Sometimes they left a place because Charles noticed that their neighbours, who had heard Mary's story, had begun to shun them; sometimes he himself noticed that Mary was in low spirits and judged that she might be better for a change. Between 1799 and 1823 they moved eight times; though never so far as to be out of easy reach of Charles's work. They made each successive dwelling, bare and shabby enough for the most part, unmistakeably their home by setting up in it certain characteristic possessions: a few pieces of worn, old-fashioned furniture which they had inherited, Charles's small, much-thumbed collection of books, also his collection of prints after Hogarth. These last, pinned to the walls, were later hung framed in narrow black, and, finally, for convenience, were bound together in a book. The Lamb's longest stay was from 1809 to 1817 at the Inner Temple near their old home. They had some happy times there; indeed, so long as Mary was well, they contrived to enjoy some happy times wherever they were living. Their pattern of life was fairly regular. Charles was at his office all day: in the evening if they were alone they read or wrote or played cards. But often they were not alone: friends, old and new, called and they generally let it be known that they would be regularly 'at home', once a week or a fortnight or a month, according to the state of Mary's health. On these evenings, the guests were entertained with whist and conversation and modest refreshments: cold meat and porter, followed later in the evening by a comforting bowl of hot punch. Often brother and sister varied their routine by going to a play: they also did a great deal of walking, exploring the London streets, where they paused at the book stalls and gazed with curiosity and amusement at the thronging crowds. On summer weekends they walked in the country, which was so close in those days to London, to enjoy the green-ness and the freshness and the silence of fields and woods. Nervously weak, the Lambs were physically strong. Though dressed so inappropriately to our eyes for country walking, they often managed to cover twelve or fifteen miles in a day, and to feel the better for it. Once or twice in the year Charles got a longer holiday and this gave the two a chance to go further afield: one summer to Oxford, another to Suffolk, but generally to the Southern coast or Southern countryside. In 1802, however, they paid a visit to Coleridge at Keswick in the Lake country, and in 1822 actually crossed the channel for a stay in Paris. This visit seems to have been no more than a moderate success. The strain of foreign travel proved too much for

GRETA HALL, KESWICK, where Charles and Mary Lamb visited Coleridge in 1802: engraving by E. Francis after a drawing by W. Westall, A.R.A.

Mary's nerves: while abroad she had a fit of madness. It was, however, only a mild one and did not last long: Charles took it with unexpected calm. Himself, he liked spending his days browsing in the open book stalls on the quays overlooking the River Seine. He also enjoyed eating frogs' legs boiled with parsley and butter, and was interested to meet Talma, the great French tragedian. But considering it was the only occasion in his whole life when Lamb left his native country, it made unexpectedly little impression on him. Afterwards, as before, the Lambs did not venture far from London.

Such was their life as it unfolds itself in the records left to us; a chronicle of homely ordinary happenings suddenly interrupted by intervals of eerie nightmare. This mixture reflected the strange discord in the spirit of Mary Lamb. Many lunatics are, as it were, of a piece: irrational, unbalanced personalities whose attacks of madness seem only the intensification of their normal condition of mind. Not so Mary Lamb; everyone who knew her agreed that the sane Mary was eminently sane. Short and square, dressed soberly but becomingly in black or dove grey, her plain face framed by a snowy, frilled cap, she gazed out at the world with a shrewd, kindly expression, now and again brightened by a smile of unusual sweetness. Her conversation confirmed the impression made by her appearance. She did not talk much; when she did it was in pleasant, quiet tones and brief, simple terms, to give her views on the subject under discussion – views candid, thoughtful and above all reasonable. Though she could not help revealing that she was intelligent and cultivated and humorous she never attempted to shine or sparkle. Yet she made a strong and favourable impression. Other people, especially women, often came to her for advice about personal problems, for they knew her judgment to be both sympathetic and realistic.

Madness brought a frightening change of personality. It was heralded by the appearance on her face of a smile not sweet but strange and disquieting: then quiet gave place to excitement, rising to frenzy in which – apparently transported to some world of her own imagining and no longer able to recognise where and who she was – she poured forth a flood of words and sentences, brilliant and extravagant but making no coherent sense. At moments she thought herself carried away, as by some time-machine, back to the age of Queen Anne and the world of Congreve's comedy, and talked in the manner of his characters, with the same glitter of wit and imagery but as if her talk had been shaken up in a verbal kaleidoscope to be confused into nonsense. If during one of these frenzied moods she fancied herself thwarted she could become dangerously violent.

The frenzied phase in her madness was followed by one of silent depression from which she would gradually emerge once again her calm, sane self with no trace left of the demon that had possessed her during her madness. This lack of connection between her sane and her insane self did make it possible for her to return to normal life more easily. It enabled her to look on her madness as having nothing to do with her real self, but rather as some infectious illness invading her from outside, which she must learn to accept, though in such a way as to cause as little trouble as possible to others – and especially to Charles.

He on his side made her welfare his first concern. His usual manner with her was relaxed and affectionately disrespectful, involving a good deal of teasing and even some friendly bickering. But people noticed that in company he was always on the watch to observe how she was feeling. If the conversation touched on a topic he thought she might find distressing 'Don't let us be sentimental!' he would say, and try to turn the subject off with a joke. We may note with amusement, too, that if Mary seemed tired he kept Coleridge away. Tactfully he explained to him: 'Consider her perpetually on the brink of madness. I think that you would almost make her dance within an inch of the precipice. She must be with duller fancies and cooler intellects!' He took for granted that her well-being depended wholly on him. 'You must die first,' he was once heard murmuring to her half-humorously. Looking at him with a smile and a reasssuring nod, she repeated, 'Yes Charles, I must die first.'

Her love for him was at times made painful for him by a fear that he did not deserve it; also that he made her troubles worse by his occasional fits of depression. This fear haunted him especially during her periods of madness when he was left alone in the house obsessedly to brood over his situation. He wrote:

When she begins to discover symptoms of approaching illness, it is not easy to say what is best to do. Being by ourselves is bad, and going out is bad. I get so irritable and wretched with her that I constantly hasten on the disorder. You cannot conceive the misery of such a foresight. I am sure that for the week before she left me, I was little better than lightheaded. I now am calm, but sadly taken down, and flat. I have however reason to suppose that this illness, like all her former ones, will be temporary; but I cannot always feel so. Meantime she is dead to me, and I miss a prop. All my strength is gone and I am like a fool, bereft of her co-operation. I dare not think lest I should think wrong; so used am I to look up to her . . . She is older, and wiser, and better than me, and all my wretched imperfections I gather to myself by resolutely thinking of her goodness.

It was because he felt so close to her that he could not hide his depressions from her. Nor could she hide her depressions from him. In a latter to a friend she comments sadly, but amusedly, on this:

It has been sad and heavy times with us lately: when I am pretty well his low spirits throw me back again; and when he begins to get a little cheerful, then I do the same kind office for him . . . You would laugh, or you would cry, perhaps both, to see us sat together, looking at each other with long and rueful faces, and saying 'how do you do?', and 'how do you do?', and then we fall a-crying and say we will be better on the morrow.

[11]

Life lived most of the time at this pitch of emotional tension could not fail to leave its mark on Charles. This was not immediately apparent: in some respects he was more like he had been as a child than are most men. Physically Charles Lamb the man was a grown-up version of Charles Lamb the boy, with a small, meagre body surmounted by a sensitive, thoughtful head with a dark skin and eyes, quick to take in whatever they lighted on, but seldom resting long on anyone or anything. Nor is he ever described as keeping still for long: even when conversing he liked to pace up and down with quick, resolute steps, snuff box or pipe in his hand – he was an incurable smoker and snuff-taker. His expression of countenance was in general grave; but gravity could suddenly give place to a fit of mirth that found vent in an outburst of laughter, or his face lit up, like his sister Mary's, by a smile of extraordinary sweetness – all the sweeter because softened by the touch of tender sadness. For the rest, he generally dressed in black: black coat, black breeches, black gaiters. This costume combined with his slight figure and light, restless movements to give him a look at once clerical and elfin.

His talk, too, was a thing of contrasts. Impeded by his stammer it spurted out in brief, concentrated sentences that often changed abruptly and unpredictably from serious to flippant, from sober truth to whimsical invention, now making a searching comment on a poem of Milton's, now rocketing up in a flight of comic fantasy, coruscating with grotesque images and preposterous plays on words. Plays on words and jokes of all sorts were scattered over his talk: in particular Lamb, like Shakespeare, could never resist an opportunity to make a pun. Often, and again like Shakespeare's, his puns were poor – at least they seem so when preserved in cold print for posterity. But at best they were puns of a high order as, when, walking down the street, he met a man carrying a hare. 'Is that your own hare?' asked Lamb, 'or do you wear a wig?' This is worthy of Lewis Carroll. Like Carroll, Lamb was a master of nonsense humour. 'Why do cats grin in Cheshire?' he exclaims suddenly in a letter, 'Because it was a County Palatine and the Cats cannot help laughing whenever they think of it, though I see not great joke in it.' Or when on one occasion he was reproved for coming late to his office he replied: 'Ah, but you must consider how early I leave.' It is to be noted that this is a joke against himself. Much of Lamb's humour – nonsensical or otherwise – makes fun of his own foibles and weaknesses. For instance, on hearing someone described as a matter-of-fact man Lamb remarked: 'I look on myself as a matter-of-lie man.' Or: 'It is unpleasant to meet a beggar; it is painful to deny him, and if you relieve him it is so much out of your pocket;' or, referring to his own lack of general knowledge: 'There is nothing I dislike so much as being alone along with a sensible, well-informed man who does not know me'; or, when asked his views on the religious education of children, 'I am determined that any children I may have shall be brought up in their father's faith – if they can find out what it is!'

There is a wistful note in this last phrase; Lamb's humour, like his smile, is sometimes touched with sadness. Also – though more rarely – with grimness; the horrifying, fascinating night fears of his childhood had struck root in his imagination so as to engender in him a taste for the macabre. This was one of the things that attracted him to the Jacobean dramatists. Like Tourneur, like Webster, like Shakespeare himself, Lamb enjoyed jokes about graveyards and coffins and suicides and hangings. It is a little disturbing to find this enjoyment in someone so tender-hearted; but it added yet another element to the rich variety of mood which made his conversation fascinating. Also famous: Charles Lamb was to become as celebrated a talker as Coleridge himself. Nor was this only for his jokes. He talked seriously as often as he talked lightly – and as memorably. Even more so, thought some of his hearers: they admired his conversation most for its power to set them thinking, for the light it could shed on a book or a man, or the complexities of human experiences. 'No-one ever stammered out such fine, deep, eloquent things in half a dozen sentences as he does,' said Hazlitt. As a matter of fact, the shimmering, shot-silk texture of Lamb's conversation shifted so incessantly from light to dark and back again that these half-a-dozen sentences were, as often as not, uttered in a tone ironical and playful. To quote Hazlitt again, 'Lamb's jests scald like tears; and he probes a question with a play of words. What a keen, laughing, hair-brained vein of homefelt truth!'

That he should make this mixed impression was nothing new. By the time he had left Christ's Hospital his paradoxical disposition had already declared itself: mirthful and melancholy, romantic and ironical, the expression of a spirit acutely aware of life's power both to delight and to hurt. He had early tried to make it his practice to meet trouble and difficulty by making light of them. In 1796, however, he had been brought face to face with an experience far too terrible for there to be any question of taking it lightly. With his own eyes he had seen the being he loved and trusted more than anyone else in the world commit an appalling act of madness and unnatural murder. Yet it had also been his experience to find he had not succumbed under the blow of this tragedy; on the contrary, he had been able to play a major part in alleviating its worst effects. Now, two years later, he had survived with his personality apparently little changed, still able to respond to life with interest and often with amusement.

Two things had made possible this extraordinary triumph over circumstances; he combined two qualities very rarely found together; an unusual taste and talent for pleasure and an extraordinary power of unselfish love. This power had given him the strength not to give way under his ordeal. He was convinced that without his support Mary would be lost; and his love for her proved a motive force strong enough to overcome any fatigue or fear that might weaken his determination to maintain that support. That he should also still enjoy life was due to his temperament; his sheer, unquenchable zest for living. He disliked the passage in Coleridge's Nether Stowey poem calling him 'gentle-hearted', partly because he thought it too flattering – 'ragged-headed, seldom-shaven, odd-eyed, stuttering would have been nearer the truth,' he said – but even more because 'gentle-hearted' suggested poor-spirited. This, Lamb rightly said, he was not. Intertwined in the subtle complexities of his nature was a strain of toughness. It was this that had made him possible to be happy at so stern a school as Christ's Hospital; it was this that now, in spite of his continual anxiety about Mary, made him able still to respond readily to the call of pleasure. Indeed, more than many luckier persons Charles Lamb found life worth living.

This was the more remarkable because his feeling was not backed by any firm faith or creed. As we have seen, during the agonies of 1796 he had longed for such a faith, and, urged by Coleridge, had tried to find one in the practices of official orthodox religion. As in earlier days, his efforts to follow these had failed. He could not find a church he felt at home in; nor had his attempts at private devotion brought him comfort. At first he blamed himself for this failure, putting it down to his own weakness and worldliness, and strove to cure himself of them. In vain; gradually, irresistibly, he found himself forced to admit, if only to himself, that religion as presented by the churches meant little to him. This was not because he was bothered by intellectual doubts. Charles Lamb never ceased to believe in God and felt deeply and instinctively out of sympathy with declared atheists. Moreover, the personality of Christ stirred in him such emotions of love and reverence that he once said that if Christ should enter a room where he was, he would be compelled to fall at his feet and kiss the hem of his garment. The trouble was that Lamb's was not in the strictest sense a religious nature: that is to say that, except in the strange brief hours after his mother's death, he never seemed to have experienced any sense of Divine Transcendent Reality beyond the show of things to which his soul might relate itself, and so find fulfilment. But he had never fully realised this lack till at the decisive crisis of his life he had turned to religion for spiritual help and failed to find it. Bit by bit this realisation sank in and he learnt to accept the fact that for him – he did not judge for others – the religion of the churches, with their accompanying apparatus of dogma and pious practices, struck no answering chord in his spirit. Gradually it began to take less part in his life. By 1800 he no longer went to church and seldom mentioned religion in his talk. If a religious topic came up in conversation Lamb would go on speaking in the same playful tone in which he spoke of other things. Walter Wilson, a pious acquaintance, once reproached him for this; he hoped, he said, that it did not mean that Lamb had become a sceptic. Apologetically Lamb wrote to him:

> Do not rashly infer, from some slight and light expressions which I may have made use of in a moment of levity in your presence, without sufficient regard to your feelings – do not conclude that I am an inveterate enemy of all religion. I have had a time of

seriousness, and I have known the importance and reality of a
religious belief. Latterly, I acknowledge, much of my seriousness
has gone off . . . but I still retain at bottom a conviction of the
truth, and a certainty of the usefulness of religion.

Paradoxically his seriousness had 'gone off' because his life had
become such a strain. With Mary liable at any time to go mad again he
must train himself to live in the moment, shutting his eyes to anything
beyond the immediate future, and to do this as cheerfully as he could
manage. Here it was that his unusual gift for enjoying himself was
such a help to him. From childhood he had learned to make the most of
any scrap of pleasure that happened to come his way. He did so all the
more ardently now that he lived under the shadow of perpetual
anxiety. Inevitably he turned first to the pleasures that were most
available – proven, everyday, homely pleasures: the pleasures of
reading favourite books, going to favourite plays, and spending
comfortable evenings in the company of old friends, enlivened by the
innocent, animal satisfactions of eating, drinking and smoking and
taking snuff. It also meant the lighter pleasures of the imagination,
whether engaged in dreamy flights of its own or transfiguring
everyday enjoyments by the play of an elfin fancy and an impish ironic
humour. These were things that Charles Lamb had always enjoyed;
but now – and this was one effect of the tension he lived under – his
enjoyment had acquired a new intensity. Just because he depended on
them as the only thing to carry him through the days with any sort of
happiness, he threw himself into them with a new abandon. In order
to forget his unsleeping anxieties, though only for an instant, his
fancies became more extravagant, his humour more freakish and
outrageous. He had always retained a strong element of the child in
his composition, and of the child's taste in fun. Now, if he felt in the
mood, he let this taste have its head. Once, entering the drawing room
at a formal party, he caught sight of a stranger's back bent over as in a
game of leapfrog. The temptation was irresistible. Coming silently up

DOVE COTTAGE, GRASMERE: watercolour drawing by Amos Green, 1806. It was from here, then known as Town End, that Wordsworth wrote to Lamb trying to persuade him to come to the Lake Country.

behind him he laid his hands lightly on the stranger's shoulders and leapfroged over him, to the amusement of a few of the company who knew him and the shocked surprise of those who did not. For Lamb did not always make a good first impression, at least not in a conventional society: his behaviour was liable to be too surprising. A light-hearted youth might be excused for suddenly leap-frogging over a total stranger's back, but not a sober-looking man apparently near the age of forty. People were also bewildered because in the company of strangers he seldom talked seriously. Instead – and especially if he felt them unsympathetic – his conversation tended to grow far more flippant and paradoxical, and sometimes outrageous to the point of impertinence. In consequence he might strike a stranger as a silly buffoon and an ill-mannered one at that.

One effect of his determination to keep up his spirits was to cause him to prefer the animated streets of London to rural solitudes, where there was nothing to distract him from his sense of his sad situation. In January 1801 he got a letter from Wordsworth inviting him to stay

COVENT GARDEN MARKET: pen and watercolour drawing by Thomas Rowlandson. 'Give me a walk in the bright piazzas of Covent Garden. I defy a man to be dull in such places'. – Lamb in a letter to Robert Lloyd.

with him in the Lake country. In Wordsworth's view there was nowhere like the Lake country for soothing a spirit under strain. Lamb disagreed. He replied:

> I ought before this to have reply'd to your very kind invitation into Cumberland. With you and your Sister I could gang anywhere. But I am afraid whether I shall ever be able to afford so desperate a Journey. Separate from the pleasure of your company, I don't care if I never see a mountain in my life. I have passed all my days in London until I have formed as many and intense local attachments, as any of you mountaineers can have done with dead nature. The lighted shops of the Strand and Fleet Street, the innumerable trades, tradesmen and customers, coaches, wagons, playhouses, all the bustle and wickedness round about Covent Garden, the very women of the Town, the Watchmen, drunken

scenes, rattles – life awake, if you awake, at all hours of the night, the impossibility of being dull in Fleet Street, the crowds, the very dirt and mud, the Sun, shining upon houses and pavements, the print shops, the old book stalls, parsons cheap'ning books, coffee houses, steams of soup from kitchens, the pantomimes, London itself a pantomime and a masquerade, – all these things work themselves into my mind and feed me, without a power of satiating me. The wonder of these sights impels me into night walks about her crowded streets, and I often shed tears in the motley Strand from fulness of joy at so much Life . . .

He added that he also loved London because he had lived there all his life, so that it was invested with the charm of the past; for him always the most powerful of charms:

My attachments are all local, purely local. I have no passion (or have had none since I was in love and then it was the spurious engendering of poetry and books) to groves and vallies. The rooms where I was born, the furniture which has been before my eyes all my life, a bookcase which has followed me about (like a faithful dog, only exceeding him in knowledge) wherever I have moved – old chairs, old tables, Streets and Squares, where I have sunned myself, my old school, – these are my mistresses. Have I not enough without your mountains? I do not envy you. I should pity you, did I not know, that the Mind will make friends of anything. Your sun and moon and skies and hills and lakes affect me no more, or scarcely come to me in more venerable characters, than as a gilded room with tapestry and tapers, where I might live with handsome visible objects. I consider the clouds above me but as a roof beautifully painted but unable to satisfy the mind, and at last, like the pictures of the apartment of a connoisseur, unable to afford him any longer a pleasure. So fading upon me from disuse, have been the Beauties of Nature, as they have been confinedly called; so ever fresh and green and warm are all the inventions of men and assemblies of men in this great city.

There were moments indeed when his memories did not always bring him happiness, when the contrast between present sorrow and remembrance of some particular past joy was so sharp as to be painful. Then he would try and dull the pain by trying to represent the past joy as having been caused by a foolish delusion. Thus when he learned in 1799 that Ann Simmons, his first love, had married another he talked to Southey about it in flippant tones, spoke of Ann laughingly as a stupid girl whom he was well rid of. Southey, recalling Lamb's romantic verses to her, was shocked at what seemed his levity. If Lamb must mention the subject, said Southey, he should not do it with 'laughing bravado'. Southey did not realise that Lamb assumed the air of bravado to hide, from others and perhaps from himself, the grief which Ann's marriage had caused him.

The same wish to make light of things encouraged his innate dislike of solemnity: solemn persons and groups of persons, solemn occasions, solemn ritual. Asked to be the godfather to a friend's child, Charles Lamb accepted out of affection, but reluctantly; he could not, he said, trust himself to behave with proper decorum during the ceremony: 'I do not like the business,' he wrote, 'I cannot muster up decorum for these occasions; I shall certainly disgrace the font . . . anything awful makes me laugh, I misbehaved once at a funeral.' Then, with one of his characteristic sudden changes of mood, he adds questioningly: 'Yet I can read about these ceremonies with proper and pious feelings. The realities of life only seem the mockeries.' His attitude to life, always ironical, had been made more so by the tragic events of 1796; for this had highlighted life's incongruities. But because these events were so terrible the quality of the irony had changed. It was now a thing of tears as well as smiles, coloured by a deep sense of the human lot, as mysterious and pathetic as well as laughable.

Lamb felt ill at ease at christenings and funerals not just because they were solemn and formal, but because they took place in church and were therefore associated with official religion, its doctrines and rituals to which, in spite of all Coleridge's eloquence, he had found himself unresponsive. All the more unresponsive now, when he had come to turn for comfort more and more to homely informal satisfactions. He shrank, even in imagination, from exiling himself from the friendly, flesh-and-blood world he lived in, to enter the awe-inspiring unearthly kingdom of Eternal Spirit, the very thought of which chilled him with a sense of fear and melancholy. The prospect of death was made more rather than less cheerful by the thought of a ghostly Hereafter, where he fancied he might find himself hankering after life on earth, even after its minor disagreeables. 'Ah!' he once said regretfully to a friend, 'we shall have none of our little quarrels and makings-up then, no questions about sixpence at whist.'

His pleasure in reading too was, if anything, more idiosyncratic than in the past. Less than ever did he care for contemporary books – though he made an exception for those written by his great friends. Charles Lamb was one of the first persons – there were not many of them at the time – to appreciate Coleridge's 'Ancient Mariner' and Wordsworth's 'Lines on re-visiting Tintern Abbey'. But even the works of Coleridge and Wordsworth he enjoyed less than those written by their sixteenth- and seventeenth-century predecessors. He loved the very look and feel of the volumes in which he read them; the shabby dog-eared little volumes of verse, the heavy folios with their parchment-coloured pages and time-stained bindings which he used to discover on the stalls of secondhand booksellers and ask the price of and save up for and at last triumphantly carry home to show to Mary and to lose himself in after supper. The folios especially won his heart; he was once seen surreptitiously kissing one containing Chapman's translation of Homer before he put it back on its shelf. He would have kissed it even more affectionately had it contained Bishop Taylor's *Holy Living* or Sir Thomas Browne's *Urn-Burial*, or Richard

Burton's *Anatomy of Melancholy*. More than ever Lamb delighted in
the neglected and supposedly odd and obscure authors of two
hundred years earlier. For him their obscurity and oddness added
attraction. As well as appealing to his taste for the grotesque, these
qualities expressed the conviction, taught him by experience, that
human life was of its nature inexplicably strange. More frivolously he
got a mischievous pleasure in surprising others by his liking for them.
One evening at a gathering of literary friends at his home the talk
turned on which of the famous dead one would have chosen to meet.
One of the guests suggested Sir Isaac Newton, another Doctor
Johnson, a third John Locke. Lamb then surprised the company by
announcing that Sir Thomas Browne and Fulke Greville, learned
poet and friend of Sir Philip Sidney, were the two worthies whom, as
he put it, he would most like 'to encounter on the floor of his
apartment in their nightgown and slippers'. Several of the company
protested, laughing at what struck them as an eccentric choice. Lamb
explained:

> The reason why I pitch upon these two authors is, that their
> writings are riddles, and they themselves the most mysterious of
> personages. They resemble the soothsayers of old, who dealt in
> dark hints and doubtful oracles; and I should like to ask them the
> meaning of what no mortal but themselves, I should suppose, can
> fathom. There is Dr. Johnson: I have no curiosity, no strange
> uncertainty about him: he and Boswell together have pretty well
> let me into the secret of what passed through his mind. He and
> other writers like him are sufficiently explicit: my friends, whose
> repose I should be tempted to disturb (were it in my power) are
> implicit, inextricable, inscrutable.
>
> When I look at that obscure but gorgeous prose-composition
> Browne's *Urn-Burial*, I seem to myself to look into a deep abyss,
> at the bottom of which are hid pearls and rich treasure; or it is like
> a stately labyrinth of doubt and withering speculation, and I

would invoke the spirit of the author to lead me through it. Besides, who would not be curious to see the lineaments of a man who, having himself been twice married, wished that mankind were propagated like trees! As to Fulke Greville, he is like nothing but one of his own Prologues spoken by the ghost of an old king of Ormus, a truly formidable and inviting personage: his style is apocalyptical, cabalistical, a knot worthy of such an apparition to untie.

Lamb's experience of life had also confirmed and intensified his admiration of the seventeenth-century playwrights, especially the tragedians Webster, Tourneur, Ford. He had long admired these as magnificent poets: now he appreciated the vision of reality which this poetry conveyed. The terrible events of 1796 had revealed to him that theirs was a true vision and that these sensational scenes of bloodshed and mania and piercing pathos and lurid horror were no outlandish fantasies but images, all too accurate, of the human condition. They disclosed, as contemporary literature did not, the realities that might even underlie the quiet-seeming existence of a poor clerk's family, like his own, living in eighteenth-century London. Charles Lamb understood these authors as few critics have done because his experience had been such as to enable him to enter into the emotions that had inspired them.

His experience also seems to have led him to enjoy the comedies of the Restoration. But for contrary reasons: if he admired the plays of Webster and Ford because he saw them as true images of tragic reality – he enjoyed those of Congreve and Wycherley because they helped him temporarily to escape from it. Most of his contemporaries had come to disapprove of them as immoral; Lamb, who delighted in them, thought that this showed his contemporaries did not understand them. They took them as pictures of the real world and judged its inhabitants accordingly. But the real world was a serious region, a battlefield of good and evil where man finds himself burdened inescapably with moral obligations and his heart inevitably moved by the sight of sin and suffering. In the world of Restoration comedy on the other hand, people have no moral obligations and no hearts. Rather is it a sort of fairyland dedicated solely to wit and sensual pleasure. To enter it, he said, was to escape into a 'Utopia of gallantry' where pleasure is duty. Reading these plays, he found, was to give himself a moral holiday and one which, as holidays should, did him good. To picture its heartless, conscienceless and exhilarating atmosphere enabled him to return strengthened and refreshed to the life of strain and anxiety in which a sad fate had decided he should live:

> I confess for myself that (with no great delinquencies to answer for) I am glad for a season to take an airing beyond the diocese of the strict conscience – not to live always in the precincts of the law-courts, but now and then, for a dream-while or so, to imagine a world with no meddling restrictions – to get into recesses, whither the hunter cannot follow me – . . . I come back to my cage and my restraint the fresher and more healthy for it. I wear my shackles more contentedly for having respired the breath of an imaginary freedom. I do not know how it is with others, but I feel the better always for the perusal of one of Congreve's – nay, why should I not add even of Wycherley's – comedies. I am the gayer at least for it, and I could never connect those sports of a witty fancy in any shape with any result to be drawn from them to imitation in real life.

Lamb also spent some of his spare time writing. During those years he composed two plays; *John Woodville*, a tragedy in the Elizabethan manner and, in a more modern style, a farce, *Mr. H*. He wrote both for his own pleasure, but also hoping that they might be put on in a theatre and so add to his income. For the same purpose he wrote papers for magazines and was later to collaborate with Mary in some

collections of tales for children. At various times during 1802 and
1804 – this time only for money – he contributed a daily humorous
paragraph to a newspaper. He did this reluctantly; and all the more
because the only time he could find time to compose these paragraphs
was before he went to work, so that his assignment involved him
forcing himself to be amusing every day at six o'clock in the morning
and before breakfast. The results of his efforts prove his reluctance to
be justified. The paragraphs are not very amusing. Nor indeed do his
other writings add much to his literary reputation. Only now and
again, in the tales for children, does his individual quality of mind and
style show themselves. Lamb had not yet discovered, in any
established literary form, prose or verse, a mode in which his genius
could manifest itself.

[III]

But he had done so, as it were unofficially, in his letters. These are
among the best things he ever wrote. They are written to a number of
persons; with a few, at one time or another, he corresponded fairly
regularly. Among these more regular correspondents were some old
friends: Coleridge, Wordsworth, Southey. Other names are Rickman,
Robert Lloyd and Thomas Manning; he came to know these later.
John Rickman was a plump, lively young man of twenty-nine in
process of making a successful career for himself as an expert in
agricultural economics. As such, he does not sound a likely friend for
Charles Lamb. But Rickman, cultivated and convivial, liked to spend
his leisure hours smoking, playing cards and in literary discussions
enlivened by flippant disrespectful jokes of a kind that appealed to
Lamb. 'A fine rattling fellow', so he described Rickman, 'who goes
through life laughing at solemn apes.' Lamb joined in the laughter.
His friendship with Rickman was founded on a common taste in
humour.

In contrast, Robert Lloyd appealed to his gentler more pensive side. He was the brother of Charles Lloyd, and, like him, was literary, hyper-sensitive and mildly in rebellion against his prosperous Quaker family; but he was easier-tempered, less egotistic and, though sometimes unreasonably depressed, less likely actually to go mad. On the contrary, his judgment of situations and character was sane and sound. Lamb noticed this. He liked Robert from the first as much as Charles: after his trouble with Charles and Coleridge he liked him better. Though he was himself still under twenty-five, his attitude to Robert was paternal: Robert confided his worries to Lamb, who listened sympathetically and gave him advice. In fatherly tones he recommended him to be careful to make friends only with the virtuous and the pious – unexpectedly he urged Robert to keep up regular religious practices – and delicately intimated that he thought he was too luckily placed to be justified in giving way to low spirits. He wrote to him:

> You say that 'this World to you seems drained of all its sweets!' At first I had hoped you only meant to insinuate the high price of Sugar! but I am afraid you meant more. O Robert, I don't know what you call sweet. Honey and the honeycomb, roses and violets, are yet in the earth. The sun and moon yet reign in Heaven, and the lesser lights keep up their pretty twinklings. Meats and drinks, sweet sights and sweet smells, a country walk, spring and autumn, follies and repentence, quarrels and reconcilements, have all a sweetness by turns. Good humour and good nature, friends at home that love you, and friends abroad that miss you, you possess all these things and more innumerable, and these are all sweet things . . . you may extract honey from everything; do not go on a gathering after gall.

He said Robert should do all he could to keep on good terms with his parents. These had, it appeared, been shocked to learn that Robert on a visit to London had been dressed in what are curiously described as a pair of 'fastidious' trousers, unseemly garments for a respectable young Quaker. They were also distressed that when at home Robert shirked attending Quaker Meetings on Sunday. It is not clear what Lamb thought about the fastidious trousers, but he strongly urged Robert to go to the Sunday Meetings: he said he would feel remorse in later life if he did not yield to what was, after all, a harmless request. But it was not in Charles Lamb to set himself consistently on the side of authority and Quakerish sobriety. Early in 1799 Robert Lloyd, in consequence of what he looked on as some unreasonable demand by his parents, escaped from home and took refuge with the Lambs. Charles Lamb backed him saying that if he stood firm the parents would be likely to give in. 'I like reducing parents to a sense of undutifulness,' he remarked mischieviously in a letter to Southey, 'I like confounding the relations of life.'

Thomas Manning, introduced to him by the Lloyds, was a more important and significant figure in Lamb's life; indeed he said that he impressed him more than anyone he had ever known, even than Coleridge. We do not know why he said this; we know too little about Manning. His few surviving letters to Lamb, though amusing, are lightweight productions designed only to entertain; and, though he had the reputation of being an enthralling talker, no-one ever recorded his talk, so that we do not know what it was like. This reputation, however, and also the story of his life, do leave us in no doubt that Manning was an unusual personality and a remarkable character – gifted, adventurous and nonconformist. The son of a Norfolk rector and early distinguished at school and Cambridge as a mathematician, he seemed all set for a successful career as cleric or academic. But both professions required him to take an oath attesting him to be a member of the Church of England and a believer in its creed. This, in spite of the disastrous effect it might have on his prospects, Manning refused to do. He had made up his mind that it was against his principles to take an oath. Instead he settled at Cambridge as a private tutor and independent scholar: but forsaking

THOMAS MANNING: plaster
copy of a marble bust by
an unknown artist

mathematics for the study of the Chinese language, a subject which, it
is easy to believe, had not hitherto attracted much attention at
England's ancient universities. Manning's interest in Chinese went
along with a more general interest in languages and in words of all
kinds: in lighter mood, he delighted in word play, in puns and
anagrams and acrostics.

This was enough to bring him and Lamb together. They met in
December 1799 and were immediately aware of an affinity of spirit.
Within a short time they were close friends, meeting when they could
and corresponding when they could not. They had other things in
common besides an interest in words: a taste for paradox and fantasy
and for convivial evenings drinking punch – 'When shall I catch a
glimpse of your honest face-to-face countenance again, or fine
dogmatical sceptical face by punch-light', wrote Lamb to him – and
in what they ate. Manning would send a present of fish or game to the

Lambs – he became a friend of Mary's too – and enjoyed going to London to eat it in their company. But shared pleasures were not the only thing that drew Lamb to Manning. At times he was conscious in himself of spiritual questionings not to be satisfied by purely materialist explanations, nor stilled by day-to-day pleasures. Half jokingly he confessed this to Manning; 'Seriously, what do you think of this life of ours? Can you make head or tail of it? How we came here, that I have some tolerable bawdy hints of; what we come here for, that I know no more than an idiot!' To such a questioning Manning was a sympathetic, comforting listener. Though he had rejected the orthodox churches, he was no materialist. There was a mystical strain in him which could show itself in his talk, though only to a few chosen persons. 'Once and once only,' wrote one of these, 'did I witness an outburst of his unembodied spirit, when such was the effect of his more than magnetic, his magic power . . . that we were all rapt and carried aloft into the Seventh Heaven.' Lamb, one of Manning's closest friends, was admitted to a glimpse of him in these visionary moments; and, though temperamentally incapable of entering into them – at no time in his life did Lamb have the sensation of being carried aloft into the Seventh Heaven – he was stirred by the personality that could have this effect on people. 'A man of Power,' so he described him, 'an enchanter almost. Far beyond Coleridge or anyone in power of impressing – when he gets you alone he can act the wonders of Egypt.' It is hard to believe that Lamb was more impressed by Manning than he had been in youth by Coleridge: but no doubt at this later period Manning, the visionary, spoke to him more convincingly than did Coleridge, the visionary; for Manning's visions, unlike those of Coleridge, were not associated with what were for Lamb the restricting chilling roles and doctrines of the official churches. Alike, then, in its spiritual and convivial aspects Manning's was a personality to raise Lamb's spirits and to chase away from him morbid terrors and grievings. 'God bless you', so ends his first letter to Lamb, 'and keep you from all evil things that walk on the face of the earth – I mean Nightmares, Hobgoblins and Spectres.'

[IV]

Manning did help to keep these unpleasant creatures away, but he was never to influence him as Coleridge once had. Lamb's character and outlook, now set into their final mature form, were no longer open to such influences. Moreover his strange and tragic situation had, as he saw it, set him apart from his fellow creatures, created a gulf between him and them too wide to be crossed by any influence. How could anyone who had not had a similar experience – and this meant all his friends – enter into the thoughts and feelings stirred in him by the hidden dark tension and despair of a life dedicated to the care of a beloved sister ordinarily wise and sane but liable suddenly to turn into a homicidal maniac! He hardly wanted anyone to try. He found he could bear his troubles more easily if he did not speak of them. Only to Mary could he open his heart. The effect of these tragic experiences was to turn Lamb, for all his easy friendliness, into a reserved man.

This appears in his letters: they contain no confessions or intimate confidences. This does not prevent them from being informal, spontaneous and personal. No letters seem less meditated or revised or designed to be studied by posterity. As we read them it is as if we were listening to him talking, we hear him pause and exclaim and interrupt himself and change his tone. Yet – and this is what gives his letters their unique quality – they never have the flatness or slovenliness of real talk. Every word is apt, every rhythm expressive, and at every turn we are met by some felicity of style. Characteristic felicities too; Lamb's racy, colloquial English, sprinkled all over with fragments of quotation and out-of-the-way, antique-sounding words and idioms, perfectly mirrored his spirit, with its curious blend of homely intimacy and delight in the archaic and fantastic.

So also does the matter of his letter echo his talk. It has the same limitations. As we have seen, he does not go in for confessions; nor does he discuss ideas or public affairs. He tells Manning:

Public affairs – except that they touch upon me and turn into private – I cannot whip up my mind to feel any interest in . . . I cannot make these present times present to me. I read histories of the past and I live in them; although, to abstract senses they are far less momentous than the noises which keep Europe awake. I am reading Burnet's *Own Times**. Did you ever read that garrulous pleasant history? . . . Burnet's good old prattle I can bring present to my mind – I can make the Revolution present to me; the French Revolution, by a converse perversity in my nature, I fling as far *from* me.

But if their matter is limited, Lamb's letters have all the variety of his ever-changing moods. Now and again, and especially when written to Manning, a letter may be a sustained piece of fanciful fooling; sometime to solemn Wordsworth or sober Southey it may consist only of thoughtful literary criticisms. More often, as in his conversation, grave and gay, tender and flippant, fantasy and irony, smiles and tears, chase one another helter-skelter across his pages with the same dazzling bewildering speed and unexpectedness as they did in his talk with his friends.

[v]

The fact that he had grown more reserved did not mean that the pleasures of friendship meant less to him. Along with literature, friendship remained a chief pleasure. Nor did the fact that he was in general more reserved than heretofore make his relations with his friends less easy and informal. Lamb was incurably informal. But, except with Mary, he was seldom intimate in the full sense of the term. No more in his talk than in his letters did he confess or confide.

* Bishop Burnet's *History of My Own Times* is about the Revolution of 1688.

ROBERT SOUTHEY:
watercolour drawing by
John Downman, 1812

Indeed, for the mature Lamb the pleasures of friendship were most characteristically enjoyed in company, in the society of a few congenial spirits who interested him or amused him in such a way as to warm his heart and take him out of himself. It was from these people were drawn the group who, when Mary was well enough, met to talk and joke and play cards and drink hot punch in whatever shabby, cosy, little living room happened to be the Lamb's home at the time.

There were old friends among them. Some of the closest, like Southey and the Wordsworths, lived far from London and could therefore only come on their rare visits. Coleridge, moving restlessly about the country and fitfully changing his mind about what to do and where to do it, was another intermittent attendant at Lamb's evenings. When he did come he made a less happy impression. A broken marriage, a growing addiction to opium, and an inability to concentrate on any project long enough to finish it, had left their mark on him. Year by year he appeared sadder, vaguer and fatter. But nothing could wholly extinguish the flame of genius that burned within him. At moments his faded eyes could still light up with the glow of inspiration, a chance remark could still start him off on a monologue which cast the old spell – especially over someone who had not known him in earlier years. Charles Lamb, inevitably, was less spellbound. But he still loved Coleridge so much that he only admitted this to others reluctantly and in qualified terms. Someone once alluded patronisingly to 'poor Coleridge.' Lamb burst out: 'Call him Coleridge. I hate 'poor' applied to such a man! I cannot bear such a man to be pitied!' And as late as 1816, when Coleridge's health and morale had sunk to their lowest point, Lamb could still remark, 'I think his essentials not touched . . . his face, when he repeats his verses, has its ancient glory; an archangel a little damaged!' This last phrase shows that Lamb had no illusions about Coleridge: there was nothing new in this; and anyway Lamb loved Coleridge all the better because he could sometimes laugh at him. 'Did you ever hear me preach?' Coleridge once asked him. 'I never heard you do anything else,' Lamb answered. And to Leigh Hunt, bewildered after an evening listening to Coleridge discoursing and rhapsodising on a theological topic, 'You must not mind Coleridge,' said Lamb mischieviously, 'he is so full of his fun!'

Other old friends often to be found at the Lambs' circle included White, cheerful impersonator of Falstaff, and George Dyer, a poverty-stricken hack writer and a friend since the early 'nineties, looking like a boney scarecrow in a rusty coat and short ragged trousers. But he delighted Lamb by his absent-mindedness. He once left the house with a coal-scuttle on his head which he had picked up by mistake for his hat. He also touched Lamb's heart by a gentleness of disposition that made him shrink instinctively from speaking ill of anyone. Lamb once asked him what he thought of a criminal recently hung for murdering two whole families. Dyer replied hesitantly, 'I think, Mr. Lamb, he must have been rather an eccentric character.'

Certainly Dyer himself was eccentric. In this he was not alone among Lamb's friends. Most of them had something odd about them and something comic, which for him added much to their likeability. Captain Burney, for instance, though a distinguished sailor and a companion of the great Captain Cook on his famous voyages to the far East, endeared himself to Lamb mainly by his taste for making puns in the language of the natives of Tahiti and for saying he enjoyed the works of Shakespeare because their author was obviously a gentleman. His son, Martin Burney, appealed to Lamb not only because he was warm-hearted and intelligent but because he was comically obstinate in argument. 'I like his obstinacy; there is something to quarrel with. One's blows do not tell upon a fellow who goes whisking about like a ball of worsted and won't stand up for his own opinions.' Lamb was also pleasantly amused by Martin Burney's apparent disinclination to wash his hands. 'Oh Martin,' he once said peering at him over the whist table, 'if dirt was trumps what a hand you would hold!'

Lamb was tolerant of Martin Burney's dirty hands because he was tolerant of human weakness in general. He liked the animal called Man and not less because he was faulty. Often his faults made him comical and for Lamb these meant more likeable. It was not that he looked down on his fellow men: he thought far too poorly of himself for that. He was very ready to admire others and enjoyed doing so. But he enjoyed laughing at them too. Best of all he liked someone like Coleridge whom he could both admire and laugh at. The people he was least inclined to like were those so consciously grave and dignified as to mind being laughed at. Even these he disliked in theory more than practice: when he did make their acquaintance he generally found something in them to please him. 'If I intend to dislike anyone,' he said, 'I'd best keep out of their company.'

His circle were drawn mostly from the middle and professional

ranks of society: academics, civil servants, journalists, art critics, a few
actors. They were more often poor than rich; a few were successful,
but more were unsuccessful. Lamb, sympathetic with human
weakness, had an especially soft spot for the unsuccessful. Even when
failure had a bad effect on a man and inclined him to sponge or soured
his temper, Lamb regarded him with an unillusioned indulgence. His
sympathy also made him sorry for persons at odds with the world
because they held religious and political views that shocked conventional opinion. Lamb's circle included a number of such persons –
Godwin, Hazlitt, Thomas Holcroft – notorious as confirmed atheists
and apostles of revolution; and this in spite of the fact that he himself
was a believing if not a practising Christian and found revolutionary
theories a subject so insufferably boring that if anyone started
discussing them in his house, he immediately chipped in to stop him.
For the rest, Lamb's friends were a mixed lot: old and young, male
and female, simple and learned, obscure and distinguished. Very
distinguished indeed so far as literature was concerned. As the years
passed one after another name to be famous in English literary history
was to be found calling on the Lambs. Of these names, Lamb knew
best William Hazlitt. Most exhilarating and perceptive of English
critics, he was not, however, an easy guest. With his sharp, dark-
featured   countenance   –   'brow-hanging,   shoe-contemplative,
strange,' Coleridge described it – he would enter a room looking as if
he suspected all those present to be his enemies. If nothing occurred
to disarm this suspicion he was apt either to maintain a sullen silence
or aggressively to pick a quarrel with anyone whom he fancied likely
to disagree with his opinions. As some of these opinions were
controversial – he supported the French and their Revolution so
passionately that he openly declared he hoped Napoleon would win
the war against England – he often achieved his quarrel. It could be an
angry quarrel. One evening at the Lambs Charles's brother John – the
Lamb brothers were now on good terms again – was so provoked by
Hazlitt's rudeness that, then and there, he knocked him down. In

contrast, if Hazlitt happened to feel the social atmosphere sympathetic, he dropped his defence to reveal a personality as exhilarating as were his writings, manifesting itself in talk glowing with imagination, alive with ideas and so generously appreciative that he would burst out in praise of the novels of Walter Scott although he knew him to be a strong opponent of the French Revolution. Indeed Hazlitt's was a divided spirit. He was born with a brilliant, active intelligence and a talent for enjoying himself as keen as Lamb's own, and more diverse: for, as well as delighting in books and plays, he was an enthusiastic amateur of prize fighting and ball games. But, alas, rooted in the very depth of his nature lay a gnawing distrustfulness of his fellow men; so that it was impossible for him to establish steady and satisfactory relations with them. An inexplicable fit of angry suspiciousness or a small difference of opinion, personal or political, was enough to turn him against an old friend and, without warning, fiercely attack him in private and in public. His relations with women were even more uncomfortable. Physically he was strongly attracted to them; but he was awkward in their company and selfish and exacting in the demands he made of them. He married twice, but both marriages were failures; nor were his extra-marital romances any more successful. Altogether Hazlitt managed during the course of his life to alienate most of his friends. The single notable exception was Charles Lamb.

The two met first in 1804 at a friend's house where they found themselves listening to a serious discussion on the subject of 'Man as he is and man as he ought to be.' 'Give me Man as he ought not to be,' interrupted Lamb frivolously. Hazlitt, who was in one of his happy moods, recognised a kindred spirit; it was the start of a lifetime's friendship. They had much in common: both loved books, both loved the theatre, both loved conversation, both laughed at the same jokes – bad jokes as well as good. In particular Hazlitt, like Lamb and the Shakespeare whom they both adored, had a weakness for facetious, over-elaborate pleasantries, especially if these were concerned with

WILLIAM HAZLITT:
chalk drawing by
William Bewick

such cheerful topics as funeral ceremonies and deaths by violence.
Indeed each was peculiarly well equipped to appreciate each other's
personality. No one has described the flavour of Lamb's conversation
more discriminatingly than Hazlitt; while Lamb judged Hazlitt to be,
along with Coleridge and Manning, the best talker he ever knew.
Though he noted his shortcomings, he did his best not to take them
seriously. Even Hazlitt's attitude to women was to Lamb a matter for
teasing rather than reproof. On one occasion he wrote:

> Hazlitt is in town. I took him to see a very pretty girl professedly,
> where there were two young girls . . . they neither laughed nor

THOMAS DE QUINCEY:
replica of a detail from a
chalk drawing by
J. Archer, 1855

sneered nor giggled nor whispered – but they were young girls –
and he sat and frowned blacker and blacker, indignant that there
should be such a thing as Youth and Beauty, till he tore me away
before supper in perfect misery and owned he could not bear
young girls. They drove him mad. So I took him home to my old
Nurse [one of Lamb's nicknames for his sister Mary], where he
recovered perfect tranquillity. Independent of this, and as I am
not a young girl myself, he is a great acquisition to us.

Always and in spite of one or two passing squabbles, Lamb
continued to consider Hazlitt an acquisition and as such to be
defended – though now and again he recognised that the best that he
could say for him was: 'Hazlitt is not a bad man; but he commits bad
actions.'

In December 1804 another man of genius entered Lamb's life. He came by way of the East India Office. There, perched upon a tall stool, Lamb looked down one day to see beneath him a delicate-featured face and small boyish figure who, in a silvery voice and with an extreme courtesy of manner, asked for Mr. Lamb. With equal courtesy Lamb scrambled down and introduced himself. The stranger said that his name was Thomas De Quincey and brought with him a letter from Coleridge. Lamb invited him to spend an evening at his home. At first it did not go smoothly, for Lamb, who was in a puckish mood, made fun of some lines in 'The Ancient Mariner', with the result that De Quincey, at this time completely under Coleridge's spell, put his hands over his ears to shut out the blasphemy. However, Mary intervened to put things right and De Quincey left the house an established friend. At once both odd and gifted, he was a man to attract Lamb. His talk was a fascinating mixture of fancy and curious learning, and expressed with a poetic eloquence. Moreover, though only nineteen years old, he had already lived a strange and adventurous life. Four years earlier, and actuated by no ascertainable motive, he had suddenly left a prosperous home and a school where he was both happy and successful, to lead a vagrant existence, at times kept secret from his family. At one time he had been hobnobbing with young peers at Eton and at another spending months, penniless and half-starved, in London, sleeping on the floor of an empty house, his only friend a sixteen-year-old prostitute for whom he cherished a romantic but platonic sentiment. At last his family discovered his whereabouts and sent him to finish his education at the university of Oxford. Thereafter he had passed his time reading and writing, and absorbing himself in flights of a visionary imagination, later to be intensified by an addiction to opium, at least as strong as Coleridge's.

Lamb never became intimate with De Quincey – he did not see him often enough – but he appreciated his company and had some admiration for his literary insight. 'Do you see that little man?' he

once asked a friend, and pointing at De Quincey, 'well – little as he is,
he has written a thing about Macbeth better than I could write. No –
not better; but I could not write anything better!' De Quincey took a
more unqualified delight in Lamb: he had a taste for the freakish and
the fanciful. He was also touched by that spirit of charity which led
Lamb so often to befriend the unpopular and the unsuccessful.

This charity was in part responsible for Lamb's friendship with
another well-known literary personality of the day, Leigh Hunt,
author and journalist. Strikingly handsome in a dark, foreign-looking
way, Hunt had a passionate and discriminating love of literature and
he expressed it in colourful talk. This talk, it is true, tended to be a
little too flowery in language, and Hunt's manner, punctuated now
and again by a tittering laugh, a little too gushing. But Lamb was not
fastidious in such matters, and he liked Hunt's company – all the
more because he knew him to be disapproved of by respectable
authority. Politically an extreme radical, Hunt published in 1812 an
article describing the Prince Regent as a 'corpulent libertine' and
'despiser of domesticities'. For these impolite words he was had up
and sentenced to no less than two years' imprisonment! It turned out
to be a mild kind of imprisonment, confinement with his family to
rooms in the gaoler's house where he could write and receive his
friends, and take the air in the gaoler's garden. Hunt seems to have
passed his time there contentedly, especially after he had his rooms
decorated with mural paintings depicting roses blooming under blue
skies. Lamb, together with Mary, used to visit him and spend pleasant
hours discussing Elizabethan literature. After Hunt left prison they
continued the same kind of conversation at their respective homes.

Sympathy with the unpopular also led Lamb to make friends with
yet another well-known man of letters, William Godwin, remembered now, if at all, as the unsatisfactory father-in-law of the poet
Shelley, but famous in his lifetime as a novelist and political theorist.
By the time Lamb got to know him Godwin's creative powers were on
the decline, but old-fashioned persons still held him in horror as a

JAMES HENRY LEIGH
HUNT: engraving by
Henry Meyer after a
painting by John Hayter,
1828

dangerous preacher of atheism and revolution. This led Lamb
instinctively to come to his defence. 'A quiet tame creature I assure
you,' he said: 'a middle-sized man both in stature and understanding.'
This is not an enthusiastic description; and in fact Lamb's feelings
about Goodwin were not enthusiastic. He found him argumentative
and humourless and tactlessly outspoken. 'I must speak freely of
people behind their backs,' Lamb once reflected. 'It is better than
Godwin's way of telling a man he is a fool to his face.' Godwin made a
habit of calling on the Lambs, but it was noted that Charles's manner
to him was never more than carefully polite.

He was polite to all his guests: but his manner to each differed
according as to how he felt about them. To Manning, for instance, it
was affectionate; to Martin Burney brotherly and familiar; with
Coleridge he was in turn mischievously teasing or deferentially

admiring; to Wordsworth he was said to be 'almost respectful'. 'Almost' seems to be the operative word, for on one occasion he suddenly addressed him as 'you rascally old Lake poet' – and even, it was rumoured, impishly tweaked his nose. Wordsworth is reported not to have minded: he always found Lamb's company exhilarating. So did the other guests, for Lamb enjoyed himself and he had the power to communicate his enjoyment to others.

Several of them have described this enjoyment: notably a lawyer and journalist called Crabb Robinson who got to know Lamb in 1806. It was Robinson's hobby to make friends with distinguished literary figures and record their talk in a diary. 'In Lamb's humble apartment,' he wrote once, 'I spent many happy hours and saw a greater number of excellent persons that I have ever seen collected together in one room.' By 'excellent' Crabb Robinson meant people who excelled intellectually and in the arts. This statement is not surprising. These evening gatherings at the Lambs' must have been among the most memorable in all English literary history; comparable to those spent at The Mermaid Tavern in the days of Shakespeare, or at The Club with Dr. Johnson and his circle. The records suggest that the quality of talk at the Lambs was unequal. The quality of its humour, for example. In their more lighthearted moments Lamb and his friends were a little too ready to laugh at any joke, bad as well as good. Moreover Lamb sometimes invited persons who did not add to the entertainment. This came partly from his taste for eccentricity: he did not sufficiently realise that eccentrics are often bores. Moreover his good nature, especially as he grew older, made him all too ready to welcome anyone who seemed to want to come, even if they were unlikely to contribute to the conversation themselves or to appreciate that of others. But in Lamb's prime and on a good evening, when one or more of the great names were there and at his best, the talk dazzled and astonished in a unique fashion – transporting its hearers into new worlds of thought and vision. Meanwhile, saving it from becoming too solemn or intense, there played ever round it the summer lightning of Lamb's sense of fun. He shone in serious talk too: he was the tutelary spirit of the whole gathering, the Puck or Ariel under whose elfin direction the diverse voices of these men of genius joined together in magical symphony. All the more magical in that it presented such a surprising contrast to its setting: the homely, friendly, shabby little gathering, with welcoming Mary in her white-frilled cap seeing to it that every guest got his or her glass of porter and cut of cold beef or pork, and where in the intervals of inspiring discussions on the nature of poetry Captain and Mrs Burney might be heard quietly commenting on the ups and downs of the rubber of whist they had just finished playing. It was this mixture of homely friendliness on the one hand, and on the other of romantic fire and fantasy, that gave the social scene at the Lamb's its distinctive charm.

[VI]

This charm, of course, was Lamb's own. That he could communicate it so effectively to his guests is a measure of his triumph over his troubles. But it was always a precarious triumph, and he knew it – knew that outside each bright, convivial gathering hovered the dreadful demons of madness threatening at any time to break in and destroy. Sometimes they did. Then, the same highly strung responsiveness that enabled Lamb to enjoy himself so intensively plunged him into an equally intense depression.

At first and before he had learned to accustom himself to Mary's recurrent attacks, depression turned to despair. In May 1800 Hetty, their old maidservant, had died: the shock of her death sent Mary into a fit of madness so acute that she could no longer be kept at home. Dazed with misery, Lamb for once turned, as in old days, to pour out his heart unreservedly to Coleridge.

I don't know why I write, except from the propensity misery has to tell her griefs. Hetty died on Friday night, about eleven o'clock, after eight days illness; Mary, in consequence of fatigue and anxiety, is fallen ill again and I was obliged to remove her yesterday. I am left alone in a house with nothing but Hetty's body to keep me company. Tomorrow I bury her, and then I shall be quite alone, with nothing but a cat to remind me that the house has been full of living beings like myself. My heart is quite sunk, and I don't know where to look for relief. Mary will get better again; but her constantly being liable to such relapses is dreadful; nor is it the least of our evils that her case and all our story is so well known around us. We are in a manner *marked*. Excuse my troubling you; but I have nobody by me to speak to me. I slept out last night, not being able to endure the change and the stillness. But I did not sleep well and I must go back to my own bed. I am going to try and get a friend to come and be with me tomorrow. I am completely shipwrecked. My head is quite bad. I almost wish that Mary were dead – God bless you! Love to Sara and Hartley. C. Lamb.

It shows the intensity of his suffering that there were moments when he almost wished Mary were dead – Mary, the being he loved best in the world. But his resilience was remarkable. Within three months he is writing again to Coleridge to say that Mary is sane again, released from confinement and that he has found a new lodging for her where their story is not known and where, for the time being at least, he is expecting them to enjoy themselves once more. 'So we are once more settled,' he says. 'I am aware that we are not placed out of reach of further interruptions; but I am determined to take what snatches of pleasure we can between the acts of our distressful drama.'

As we have seen, he succeeded in his determination, managing to enjoy much of his life in spite of Mary's recurrent periods of madness. All the same, the strain of a life lived on the brink of tragedy could not fail to affect his nerves. This showed often in the febrile nature of his gaiety, in his startling changes of mood. If his nerves were under an extreme strain his spirits suddenly dropped so that he sat sunk in a silence from which nothing could raise him. More rarely and uncharacteristically, he could grow irritable, surprising people by answering them sharply and impolitely: he would even snap at Mary. This meant less; he was too close to her to keep on his good behaviour if he did not feel like it. For the same reason Mary took his outbursts easily enough. She realised what he was feeling and knew how to deal with it. In such moments she resumed her old role of maternal elder sister, reassuring and tranquilising and wise.

Other people found her the same. The part she played in the Lamb circle was not confined to seeing that the room was comfortable and supervising refreshments. Her personality was an individual and essential element in creating the Lambs' social atmosphere; an element of calm and kindly good sense to balance her brother's freakishness and fantasy. The flavour of this personality comes across to us in her letters, notably in those she wrote to a young woman-friend called Sarah Stoddart, later to marry William Hazlitt. Miss Stoddart's personal life seemed to have been confused and worrying. In 1803, for instance, she confides to Mary that though officially engaged to a Mr. Turner, she now finds herself hankering after an earlier admirer called William. She is also concerned because her brother has married a woman with whom she does not feel at ease. Mary replied:

My dear Sarah,
I returned home from my visit yesterday, and was much pleased to find your letter; for I have been very anxious to hear how you are going on. I could hardly help expecting to see you when I came in; though I should have rejoiced to have seen your merry face again . . . The terms you are upon with your Lover does (as you say it will) appear wondrous strange to me; however, as I cannot enter into your feelings, I certainly can have nothing to say to it, only that I sincerely wish you happy in your own way, however

odd that way may appear to me to be. I would begin now to advise
you to drop all correspondence with William; but, as I said before,
as I cannot enter into your feelings and views of things, *your ways
not being my ways*, why should I tell you what I would do in your
situation? So, child, take thy own ways, and God prosper thee in
them!

One thing my advising Spirit must say – use as little *Secrecy* as
possible; and, as much as possible, make a friend of your sister-in-
law – you know I was not struck with her at first sight; but, upon
your account, I have watched and marked her very attentively;
and, while she was eating a bit of cold mutton in our kitchen, we
had a serious conversation. From the frankness of her manner, I
am convinced she is a person I could make a friend of; why should
not you? We talked freely about you: she seems to have a just
notion of your character, and will be fond of you, if you will let
her.

In this passage we seem to hear the very tone of Mary's voice, voicing
opinions frank and outspoken but so warm with affectionate good
sense that they could not have given offence.

[VII]

Certainly she never offended Charles. Was it not to her to whom he
turned for comfort when he felt depressed, on whom he depended to
intervene and smooth things over on the few occasions when he
showed himself irritable and sharp-spoken in company. More often
she intervened to check him from drinking too much. Here it was that
the nervous strain under which he lived declared itself more often and
most noticeably: for it attacked him where he was most vulnerable.
On the one hand he was convivial and welcomed strong drink as
adding to his enjoyment; on the other hand he was highly-strung and
liable to attacks of melancholy and shyness; so that he turned to
alcohol to cheer him up and give him courage. These various causes

had made him a regular drinker ever since he grew up and, as we have seen, he was sometimes half-tipsy. How much more did he feel the need of drink after the tragedy of his mother's death and under the continual threat of another attack of Mary's madness!

In 1800 his drinking habits were further strengthened by his excursion into popular journalism. This led him into a tougher world where he made friends with a pair of hard-drinking, dissipated journalists called Fell and Fenwick. He spent evenings with them when, in order to feel at ease in their boisterous company, he drank a great deal more than he was used to. This association did not last long: financial troubles seem to have driven Fell and Fenwick out of London; and in any case Lamb began to discover that the better he knew them the less he found in common with them. But he had acquired in their company the habit of drinking more than before: he now did so even with old friends like Manning and the Lloyd brothers. From this time on all too often Lamb ended a convivial evening far from sober, unless Mary was there tactfully to restrain him.

Alas, she was not always able to be there. Either he was at an all-male party or – worse still – she was away, shut up in a madhouse sometimes for weeks on end. It was no wonder that in these circumstances he drank too much in order to dull his misery. In fact, it increased it; for when he was sober again he felt guilty and ashamed as well as depressed. From time to time he tried to cut down his drinking and even to stop it altogether; also to give up smoking which, he said, encouraged him to drink. He found that the relaxed ease of spirit induced by nicotine fatally weakened his determination to restrain himself. His efforts to resist temptation, however, never lasted long. Soon he began drinking again, and soon remorse induced by this new evidence of his weakness reawoke his feelings of guilt. These, in their turn, disappeared to give place to a characteristic lightning change of mood in which he would refer to his drunken evenings light-heartedly enough.

It is questionable whether he needed to feel so very guilty. He
might seem to, if we are to judge the matter by the lamenting,
conscious-stricken references to his drinking which now and again
appear in his letters; still more by a sensational piece entitled
'Confessions of a Drunkard', published in 1812 and which many of
his acquaintances took a shocked pleasure in believing to be
autobiographical. Lamb denied this: and he was justified in doing so;
for, though we can recognise some of it as drawn from his experience,
in the main it is fiction. The confessing drunkard, who is its narrator,
represents himself as a confirmed tragic alcoholic sunk into a state
where he can neither enjoy himself or be of use to anyone else,
whereas throughout these years Lamb was able both to take good care
of Mary and to do his work at the East India office to the satisfaction of
his employers. Moreover his friends never spoke of his drinking as
doing him any harm physically or morally. On the contrary, they
found the spectacle of Lamb in his cups more entertaining than
distressing. Of course, people in those days looked leniently on
drunkenness as a form of enjoyment which any man might be allowed
to indulge in now and again. Even when Lamb and Manning, on one
evening at Charles Lloyd's, kept poor Mrs. Lloyd, who had lately
given birth to a child, awake till three in the morning by merrily
shouting and laughing in the room below, they did not come in for
much blame.

As a matter of fact, Lamb seldom made a nuisance of himself in this
way. For one thing it was seldom that he drank enough to do so. He
had a weak head which showed the effects of alcohol after two glasses
of wine, and though he rarely confined himself to two glasses, it was
only now and again that he drank very heavily. It may not have, in
consequence, been very good for his health but it did not impair his
efficiency. Neither did it change his personality for the worse: no
description of him in his cups presents him as disgusting or
quarrelsome or embarrassingly sentimental. Rather, he was an
exaggeration of his sober self in high spirits – drunk with an airy elfin

drunkenness that grew ever more freakish and fantastic, more prone
to extravagant unexpected talk and actions, punctuated by sudden fits
of falling asleep. Let De Quincey describe one of these:

> Over Lamb, at this period of his life, there passed regularly, after
> taking wine, a brief eclipse of sleep. It descended upon him as
> softly as a shadow. In a gross person, laden with superfluous flesh,
> and sleeping heavily, this would have been disagreeable; but in
> Lamb, thin even to meagreness, spare and wiry as an Arab of the
> desert, or as Thomas Aquinas wasted by scholastic vigils, the
> affection of sleep seemed rather a network of aerial gossamer than
> of earthly cobweb – more like a golden haze falling upon him
> gently from the heavens than a cloud exhaling upwards from the
> flesh. Motionless in his chair as a bust, breathing so gently as
> scarcely to seem certainly alive, he presented the image of repose
> midway between life and death, like the repose of sculpture; and,
> to one who knew his history, a repose affectingly contrasting with
> the calamities and internal storms of his life. I have heard more
> persons that I can now distinctly recall observe of Lamb when
> sleeping that his countenance in that state assumed an expression
> almost seraphic, from its intellectual beauty of outline, its child-
> like simplicity, and its benignity. It could not be called a
> transfiguration that sleep had worked in his face; for the features
> wore essentially the same expression when waking; but sleep
> spiritualized that expression, exalted it, and also harmonized it.
> Much of the change lay in that last process. The eyes it was that
> disturbed the unity of effect in Lamb's wakened face. They gave a
> restlessness to the character of his intellect, shifting like Northern
> Lights, through every mode of combination with fantastic
> playfulness, and sometimes by fiery gleams obliterating for the
> moment that pure light of benignity which was the predominant
> reading on his features. . . . On awaking from his brief slumber,
> Lamb sat for some time in profound silence and then, with the

most startling rapidity, sang out – 'Diddle, diddle, dumpkins' . . . not looking at me, but as if soliloquizing. For five
minutes he relapsed into the same deep silence; from which again
he started up into the same abrupt utterance of 'Diddle, diddle
dumpkins.' I could not help laughing aloud at the extreme energy
of this sudden communication, contrasted with the deep silence
that went before and followed. Lamb smilingly begged to know
what I was laughing at, and with a look of as much surprise as if it
were I that had done something unaccountable and not himself . . .

On more festal evenings when Lamb drank more he did not wake
up from his sleep so easily. Then one of his friends might have to put
him to bed or, if he were away from home, carry him back there on his
back, his countenance still relaxed in a child-like seraphic smile. Next
morning he was likely to wake up feeling, temporarily at least,
ashamed of himself. All the more as the years passed and he realised
that the middle-aged man drunk is an unseemly spectacle. Even on
such mornings, however, he was generally able to go off to his office at
the usual time and to do his work there. Altogether Lamb's friends
were right in regarding his drinking bouts as no very deplorable
affairs; and, considering the strain in which he was living, they were
understandable.

CHAPTER II : ELIA AND BEFORE

Between 1799 and 1825 then, the general pattern of Charles Lamb's life did not alter. But within that pattern the course of his literary and personal story was diversified now and again by an event. The literary events, most of them, were not such as to give him much satisfaction. He wanted to be a creative writer, but what with his work and his friends he found it hard to concentrate steadily enough on his writing to get anything substantial finished. To meet this difficulty in 1806 he hired a room in a neighbouring house for two hours every evening to which he might retire in order to work undisturbed. It proved no use. Within a week or two he was back home to tell Mary that writing away from home made him feel unpleasantly lonely and no more able to concentrate than before. But even if he had concentrated it is improbable that the result would have been worth the effort. Over the years he did manage to finish a few poems and prose pieces but they did not win him any reputation, for at best they were no more than pleasant.

More successfully, and in order to add to their modest income, he collaborated with Mary in some books for children; *Tales from Shakespeare*, *The Adventure of Ulysses*, and some stories for girls, *Mrs Leicester's School*. Of these the *Tales from Shakespeare* were a success: they achieved the status of a children's classic and continued to be reprinted for at least a century. This is a little surprising; for the tales are told in a gentle undramatic manner, unlikely, one would have thought, to excite children in Lamb's day, let alone many years later. The same is true of *The Adventures of Ulysses*; less so of *Mrs Leicester's School*, a collection of tales supposed to be related to one another by the members of a girls' school, and telling of happenings drawn from within their own experience. They are naif little anecdotes, each complete with a simple moral then demanded of books specifically designed to be read by children. Those written by Charles – there are three of them – are as naif as any, but hints of his individual imaginative quality are faintly perceptible in them – in particular his romantic feeling for the ancient and picturesque, for faded, ancient folios and grey, gargoyled old village churches. At moments, too, the cosy and comfortable atmosphere of the stories is unexpectedly chilled by a breath of fear and of sadness. One story, 'The Witch Aunt,' recalls the night fears of his own childhood, another, 'Arabella Hardy,' ends with the death of the gentle sailor who cares so tenderly for the five-year-old heroine in her voyage home through stormy seas alone with a crew of rough seamen.

Lamb was even less successful as a playright than as a storyteller. During these years he made efforts to get both his tragedy *John Woodville* and his farce *Mr H*, published. *John Woodville* was rejected; *Mr H* was accepted – much to Lamb's delight. In the event it fared the worse of the two. It was produced at Drury Lane on December 10, 1806. The evening started auspiciously: a crowd of relations and friends had gathered to support it including Mary and John Lamb, Hazlitt, Crabb Robinson and a large number of fellow clerks from the East India Office who came to encourage their popular colleague. The prologue, also written by Lamb, was loudly applauded. But soon after the play began some hisses were heard; as the play proceeded this settled down into a loud, unceasing hiss from all over the theatre. Lamb looked round, accepted the situation, and joined in the hissing. 'I did so,' he explained afterwards, 'because I was so damnably afraid of being recognised as the author.' Speaking of it afterwards, he admitted his disappointment, but was careful to do so and to describe the scene which occasioned it with a light humorous exaggeration which indicated that he did not take it too seriously. He wrote to Manning:

Damn 'em how they hissed! It was not a hiss neither, but a sort of a frantic yell, like a congregation of mad geese, with roaring sometimes like bears, mows and mops like apes, sometimes snakes, that hiss'd me into madness. 'Twas like St. Anthony's

THE NEW DRURY LANE THEATRE from the stage: engraving published by Richard Phillips, 1804. This is the theatre in which Lamb's *Mr. H* was produced.

temptations. Mercy on us but that God should give his favourite children, men, mouths to speak with, to discourse rationally, to promise smoothly, to flatter agreeably, to encourage warmly, to counsel wisely, to sing with, to drink with and to kiss with: and that they should turn them into mouths of adders, bears, wolves, hyenas and whistle like tempests, and emit breath through them like distillations of aspic poison, to asperse and vilify the innocent labours of their fellow creatures who are desirous to please them.

It was hard on Lamb that the audience should have hissed so very loudly, but understandable that they did not much enjoy the play. *Mr H* is a thin little piece whose single and central incident is that the heroine breaks off her engagement when she discovers that her fiancé's name – hitherto hidden from her – is Hogsflesh. This – comic enough as so far as it goes – is not enough to sustain an hour-long theatrical entertainment. The truth was that Lamb was no more a dramatist than he was a storyteller. He had yet to find the right literary mode in which his creative impulse could express itself.

This was not true of his critical impulse. In 1808, the same year as *Mrs Leicester's School*, he published a volume entitled *Characters of Dramatic Writers Contemporary with Shakespeare*, an anthology of brief extracts from the Elizabethan and Jacobean tragedians, who, he thought, were wrongfully neglected: notably Marlowe, Webster, Heywood and Ford. Each piece was followed by a passage of critical appreciation. The book is a highly characteristic production, fragmentary, impressionistic, idiosyncratic and more concerned to convey Lamb's personal reaction to the piece discussed than to deliver a balanced judgement on it. This leads him now and again to make very extreme statements, as when he says that the death scene in Marlowe's *Edward II* 'moves pity and terror beyond any scene ancient or modern with which I am acquainted'. But the book does reveal Lamb the critic at his best: original, penetrating, and with a subtle power to discriminate the precise qualities which gives the work he is talking about its unique flavour, and able to describe this flavour with an apt and evocative phrase, as when he says of the dirge in Webster's *White Devil*:

> I never saw anything like the funeral dirge in this play, for the death of Marcello, except the ditty which reminds Ferdinand of his drowned father in *The Tempest*. As that is of the water, watery; so this is of the earth, earthy. Both for that intentness of feeling, which seems to resolve itself into the element which it contemplates.

Nor, though so brief, were Lamb's criticisms slight. For him the plays taught man about life: had he not himself learned from personal experience that their strange wild stories were images all too true of tragic reality. Moreover he saw them as revealing this reality in an impressive moral context. 'My leading design,' he said, 'was to illustrate what may be called the moral sense of our ancestors . . . to show in what manner they failed when they placed these by the power of imagination in trying circumstances': he found their pictures of human virtue convincing and beautiful in such a way that they must surely inspire readers to try and imitate them. For to Lamb, as these Elizabethan writers, the highest literature was marked by its power to promote human virtue. He tells his child readers in his preface to his *Tales from Shakespeare* that these plays should be to them: 'enrichers of the fancy, strengtheners of virtue, a withdrawing of self and mercenary thoughts, a lesson of sweet and honourable thoughts and actions to teach you courtesy, benignity, generosity and humanity.'

[11]

The events of these years marking Lamb's personal, as contrasted with his literary life story, were concerned with his friendships and consist mainly of the successive entry into his life of new friends: Hazlitt and De Quincey in 1804, Rickman in 1805, Crabb Robinson in 1806 to mention only a few of them. These were contemporaries to be treated on equal terms. A few years later came a whole group of younger friends: Thomas Talfourd, Brian Proctor, Bernard Barton, Thomas Hood and Peter Patmore. All these, and notably Thomas Hood, were professional or occasional writers. It was the literary strain in them that drew them to Lamb. Each in his turn met him and was immediately fascinated by his talk and showed it. As they got to know him better and became aware of the unselfish sweetness of his character, especially as it showed itself when he was with Mary, their admiration warmed into love. In return Lamb grew fond of them and gave them affectionate paternal advice about their lives and their writings.

New friends, however, whether young or old, never meant as much to him as Coleridge and Manning had done; and still did when he saw

them. This was not so much as it once had been. Coleridge for a large
part of the time was out of London; when he was there, he visited the
Lambs' less often than in the past. This neglect, it is hardly necessary
to say, was not deliberate. Rather was it that the opium-hazed
confusion in which he passed his days made him unable to keep up a
steady relationship with anyone. Very different reasons separated
Manning from Lamb. The study of the Chinese language had led him
to take a deep interest in Chinese civilization, so much so that he
decided to go and investigate it on the spot. Accordingly, and in order
to prepare himself, in 1801 he left London for Paris, at that time
apparently noted for its Chinese studies. This was during the
precarious Peace of Amiens; one day Manning got a chance of seeing
Napoleon himself; he described him enthusiastically to Lamb as
having a 'god-like' face set off by a simple blue uniform. 'What God'
asked Lamb. 'Mars or Bacchus or Apollo, or the god Serapis fleeing
from the fury of the dog Anubis?' He added that he heard that
Napoleon was very small, even smaller than himself. Lamb's flippant
tone, as elsewhere in this correspondence, concealed a wistful
sadness, this because Manning with his peculiar power to cheer and
exhilarate him should be leaving for distant lands – especially as they
were so very distant. At one moment, so he told Lamb, Manning had
thought of visiting Independent Tartary. Lamb commented:

> The general scope of your letter afforded no indications of
> insanity; but some particular points raised a scruple. For God's
> sake don't think any more of Independent Tartary . . . my dear
> friend, think what a sad pity it would be to bury such parts (as
> yours) in heathen countries among nasty, unconversible, horse-
> belching Tartar people! some say they are cannibals; and then
> conceive a Tartar fellow eating my friend and adding the cool
> malignity of mustard and vinegar!

Whether or not from fear of cannibals, Manning dropped the idea of visiting Tartary, but he remained determined to go to China. He came back to England to make final preparations for his journey. In May 1806 he set sail. Before his going Lamb and he exchanged characteristic letters of farewell. Lamb writes:

O Manning, I am serious to sinking almost, when I think that all those evenings, which you have made so pleasant, are gone perhaps for ever. Four years you talk of, maybe ten, and you may come back and find such alterations! Some circumstance may grow up to you or to me, that may be a bar to the return of any such intimacy . . . indeed we die many deaths before we die, and I am almost sick when I think that such a hold as I had of you is gone. I have friends, but some of them are changed. Marriage, or some circumstance, rises up to make them not the same. But I felt sure of you. And that last token you gave me of expressing a wish to have my name joined with yours, you know not how it affected me: like a legacy. God bless you in every way you can form a wish. May He give you health, and safety, and the accomplishment of all your objects, and return you again to us, to gladden some fireside or other (I suppose we shall be moved from the Temple).

Manning answered:

As we have not sailed yet, & I have a few minutes, why should not I give you a line to say that I received your kind letter yesterday, & shall read it again before I have done with it. I am sorry I had not time to call on Mary – but I didn't call even on my own father; & he's 70 & loves me like – a father . . . I am not dead nor dying – some people go into Yorkshire for 4 years & never come to London all the while! I go to China. What's the difference to our London friends? I am persuaded I shall come back & see more of you than I have been able. Who knows but I may make a fortune & take you & Mary out a-riding in my Coach.

Manning was away for twelve years; years crammed with as much novelty and adventure as he could possibly have wished. After spending some time in Canton and Calcutta he started out, alone but for one servant, for Thibet and got as far as the Holy City of Lhasa, the first European ever to have set foot there. Returning to China, he acted for a time as interpreter in Eastern languages to the British Ambassador in Peking. At last in 1816 he started home; but he managed on the way to call at St. Helena, where he had several interesting talks with Napoleon, now held prisoner there. Whether Manning thought that he still looked 'god-like' is not reported. December 1817 found him back in England, bronzed, bearded, reputed to be the greatest living expert on China and the Chinese and all primed, it must have seemed, to produce some work that would make him famous. Unaccountably, however, he produced little. Indeed the rest of his life was to be an anticlimax and he himself restless, reclusive and a little embittered.

Except when he was with Lamb: their relationship was as pleasurable as ever. Moreover in tone it was unaltered. Surprisingly, it had been so throughout Manning's absence. Now and again, though not often, the two wrote to each other. When they did they hardly referred to Manning's new and extraordinary experiences: the name of Lhasa was not, so far as we know, mentioned in their correspondence. Instead, as when they were still in England, these letters were brilliant exhibitions of fantasy and nonsense and wit and near poetry, but with hardly any news in them. Manning cannot have minded this, for news or no news, Lamb's letters to him did convey the full impact of his personality at its most entertaining. Reading them Manning must have felt that Lamb had suddenly entered his room and was talking to him. One needs to read any one letter as a whole to get its full effect: here are a few typical sentences taken from several letters to suggest their flavour:

When I last wrote to you, I was in lodgings. I am now in

chambers. No. 4 Inner Temple Lane, where I should be happy to see you any evening. Bring any of your friends, the Mandarins, with you . . . My best room commands a court, in which there are trees and a pump, the water of which is excellent – cold with brandy, and not very insipid without. Here I hope to set up my rest, and not quit till Mr. Powell, the undertaker, gives me notice that I may have possession of my last lodging. He lets lodgings for single gentlemen.

I have published a little book for children on titles of honour: and to give them some idea of the difference of rank and gradual rising, I have made a little scale, supposing myself to receive the following various accessions of dignity from the king, who is the fountain of honour – as at first, 1, Mr. C. Lamb; 2, C. Lamb, Esq.; 3, Sir C. Lamb, Bart.; 4, Baron Lamb of Stamford; 5, Viscount Lamb; 6, Earl Lamb; 7, Marquis Lamb; 8, Duke Lamb. It would look like quibbling to carry it on further, and especially as it is not necessary for children to go beyond the ordinary titles of sub-regal dignity in our own country, otherwise I have sometimes in my dreams imagined myself still advancing, as 9th, King Lamb; 10th, Emperor Lamb; 11th, Pope Innocent, higher than which is nothing but the Lamb of God.

It is New-Year here. That is, it was New-Year half a-year back, when I was writing this. Nothing puzzles me more than time and space, and yet nothing puzzles me less; I never think about them.

Wordsworth, the great poet, is coming to town; he is to have apartments in the Mansion House. He says he does not see much difficulty in writing like Shakespeare, if he had a mind to try it. It is clear, then, nothing is wanting but the mind.

During these later years, Lamb made new acquaintances as well as new friends. Three of these are interesting enough in themselves to deserve special mention. The first was John Clare, the Northampton-shire peasant poet whose fresh and lovely verses have only come to be fully appreciated in our own time. Rustic and ingenuous, Clare only met Lamb a few times on his occasional visits to London. But he responded immediately and intensely to Lamb's charm – if they had seen each other often they would certainly have become great friends. Clare listened enraptured to Lamb's talk and composed two sonnets in his honour. The second new acquaintance, Benjamin Robert Haydon, cuts a conspicuous figure in the literary and artistic records of the age as a failed ambitious painter, an enthralling autobiographer, and a personality at once impressive and preposterous. The third of the trio achieved a different and less enviable kind of fame. Thomas Wainewright was a dandified artist-journalist who got to know Lamb through the *London Magazine* and appealed to his taste for lively colourful personalities: he once described Wainewright as 'kindly and light-minded'. The first epithet seems to have been misapplied: for in his later years, and after Lamb's death, Wainewright was tried for his life and proved to be certainly a forger and probably a poisoner. He was transported and ended his days as a convict in Van Diemens Land. It is amusing to speculate how Lamb, had he lived long enough to follow his subsequent career, would have felt about Wainewright. Most men would have turned against him; but with Lamb one cannot be certain. He might have taken a whimsical pleasure in remaining friends with a possible poisoner.

Wider acquaintance went along with a wider social life. Lamb's reputation as a talker led him to be often invited out to dinner. One such occasion was a dinner at Haydon's who described it thus:

> In December Wordsworth was in town, and as Keats wished to know him I made up a party to dinner of Charles Lamb, Wordsworth, Keats and Monkhouse, his friend; and a very pleasant party we had.

BENJAMIN ROBERT
HAYDON:
self-portrait

I wrote to Lamb, and told him the address was '22, Lisson Grove, North, at Rossi's, half way up, right hand corner.' I received his characteristic reply.

My dear Haydon,
   I will come with pleasure to 22, Lisson Grove, North, at Rossi's, half way up, right hand side, if I can find it.
                        Yours,
                           C. Lamb.
20, Russel Court,
   Covent Garden East,
      half way up, next the corner,
         left hand side.

On December 28th the immortal dinner came off in my painting room. Wordsworth was in fine cue, and we had a glorious set-to, –

on Homer, Shakespeare, Milton and Virgil. Lamb got exceed-
ingly merry and exquisitely witty; and his fun in the midst of
Wordsworth's solemn intonations of oratory was like the sarcasm
and wit of the fool in the intervals of Lear's passion. He made a
speech and voted me absent, and made them drink my health.
'Now,' said Lamb, 'you old lake poet, you rascally poet, why do
you call Voltaire dull?' We all defended Wordsworth, and
affirmed there was a state of mind when Voltaire would be dull.
'Well,' said Lamb, 'here's Voltaire – the Messiah of the French
nation, and a very proper one too.'

He then, in a strain of humour beyond description, abused me
for putting Newton's head into my picture – 'a fellow,' said he,
'who believed nothing unless it was as clear as the three sides of a
triangle.' And then he and Keats agreed he, Newton, had
destroyed all the poetry of the rainbow by reducing it to the
prismatic colours. It was impossible to resist him, and we all

JOHN KEATS:
pencil drawing by
Charles Brown, 1819

drank 'Newton's health, and confusion to mathematics'. It was delightful to see the good-humour of Wordsworth in giving in to all our frolics without affectation and laughing as heartily as the best of us.

By this time other friends joined, amongst them poor Ritchie who was going to penetrate by Fezzan to Timbuctoo. I introduced him to all as 'a gentleman going to Africa'. Lamb seemed to take no notice; but all of a sudden he roared out, 'Which is the gentleman we are going to lose?' We then drank the victim's health, in which Ritchie joined.

In the morning of this delightful day, a gentleman, a perfect stranger, had called on me. He said he knew my friends, had an enthusiasm for Wordsworth and begged I would procure him the happiness of an introduction. He told me he was a comptroller of stamps, and often had correspondence with the poet. I thought it a liberty; but still, as he seemed a gentleman, I told him he might come.

When we retired to tea we found the comptroller. In introducing him to Wordsworth I forgot to say who he was. After a little time the comptroller looked down, looked up and said to Wordsworth, 'Don't you think, sir, Milton was a great genius?' Keats looked at me, Wordsworth looked at the comptroller. Lamb who was dozing by the fire turned round and said, 'Pray, sir, did you say Milton was a great genius?' 'No, sir; I asked Mr. Wordsworth if he were not.' 'Oh,' said Lamb, 'then you are a silly fellow.' 'Charles! my dear Charles!' said Wordsworth; but Lamb, perfectly innocent of the confusion he had created, was off again by the fire.

After an awful pause the comptroller said, 'Don't you think Newton a great genius?' I could not stand it any longer. Keats put his head into my books. Ritchie squeezed in a laugh. Wordsworth seemed asking himself, 'Who is this?' Lamb got up, and taking a candle, said, 'Sir, will you allow me to look at your phrenological development?' He then turned his back on the poor man, and at every question of the comptroller he chaunted –

'*Diddle diddle dumpling, my son John*
  Went to bed with his breeches on.'

The man in office, finding Wordsworth did not know who he was, said in a spasmodic and half-chuckling anticipation of assured victory, 'I have had the honour of some correspondence with you, Mr. Wordsworth.' 'With me, sir?' said Wordsworth, 'not that I remember.' 'Don't you, sir? I am a comptroller of stamps.' There was a dead silence; – the comptroller evidently thinking that was enough. While we were waiting for Wordsworth's reply, Lamb sung out

'*Hey diddle diddle*
  The cat and the fiddle.'

'My dear Charles!' said Wordsworth, –

'*Diddle diddle dumpling, my son John,*'

chaunted Lamb, and then rising, exclaimed, 'Do let me have another look at that gentleman's organs.' Keats and I hurried Lamb into the painting-room, shut the door and gave way to inextinguishable laughter. Monkhouse followed and tried to get Lamb away. We went back but the comptroller was irreconcilable. We soothed and smiled and asked him to supper. He stayed though his dignity was sorely affected. However, being a good-natured man, we parted all in good-humour, and no ill effects followed.

All the while, until Monkhouse succeeded, we could hear Lamb struggling in the painting-room and calling at intervals, 'Who is that fellow? Allow me to see his organs once more.'

It was indeed an immortal evening. Wordsworth's fine intonation as he quoted Milton and Virgil, Keats's eager inspired look, Lamb's quaint sparkle of lambent humour, so speeded the stream of conversation, that in my life I never passed a more delightful time.

One cannot help feeling a little sorry for the poor comptroller of stamps. Lamb's behaviour does suggest that this was an evening when he was flown with drink. However, Haydon does not say that he was, but only in unusually and delightfully high spirits. If so, this is more evidence of the childlike strain in him surviving to middle age in spite of his troubles.

At another party Lamb certainly did drink too much. Once again the guests were distinguished writers including Coleridge and Wordsworth, together with a poet of a different kind and from a different social circle, Thomas Moore, man of fashion and friend of Byron. He had not met Lamb before. 'I can still recall to my mind,' reports Crabb Robinson, another guest, 'the look and tone with which Lamb addressed Moore when he could not articulate very distinctly: 'Mr. Moore – will you drink a glass of wine with me?' – suiting the action to the words . . . then he went on, 'Mr. Moore till now I have always felt an antipathy to you; but now that I have seen you I shall like you ever after.'

Moore, in his journals, said he enjoyed meeting Lamb: 'A clever fellow who said some excellent things.' But he added that he regretted Lamb's villainous and abortive puns'.

[III]

Yet beneath his childlike and uninhibited surface Lamb remained deeply reserved and so able to surprise people, both then and now, by an unexpected act. This happened in 1819. Lamb had always continued to be a keen theatre goer and amateur of the art of acting, just as ready to be enthusiastic about the stage stars of his middle life – Munden and Liston, Kean and Charles Kemble – as he had been about those of his youth. By 1817 he had begun to take a particular pleasure to the performances of a leading actress called Fanny Kelly. Round-faced and plumpish, she did not owe her success to her looks. But she radiated a warm, friendly charm and was a versatile

FRANCES MARIA [FANNY] KELLY: engraving by Thomson after a painting by William Derby, 1823

performer, equally skilled to rouse laughter or tears in her audience, equally convincing as a rustic English milkmaid and as an elderly gypsy fortune teller, and in both identifying herself so completely with each role as to seem wholly unaware of the audience who was watching her. Her performances were especially distinguished by 'naturalness', a quality which especially appealed to Lamb. He took every chance of praising her publicly both in prose and verse, and in private rhapsodised to his friends about the 'divine plain face of Miss Kelly'. It was not long before he managed to meet her and to discover that he liked the woman as much as he admired the actress. Indeed she sounds both likeable and interesting. The daughter of an impoverished mother deserted by her husband, Fanny Kelly had from her early years helped to support her family as a child actress, and had since managed to work her way up to the top of the theatrical tree without acquiring any of the characteristic faults of her tough and competitive profession. The twenty-five-year-old Fanny Kelly was unegotistic, untemperamental, did not show off and had a reputation for charity. Away from the stage, she appeared an unaffected, pleasant-mannered lady, 'calm, sensible, warm-hearted' said Crabb Robinson – with no obvious trace of the actress about her. She was also humorous and intelligent, well able to hold her own in conversation at an evening with the Lambs, and keen enough to improve her mind to ask Mary to give her some lessons in Latin. By 1818 she was accepted as a regular member of their circle. Mary took to her; Charles delighted in her, and felt her a sympathetic spirit able to appreciate his more characteristic and zany vein of humour. 'I am the worst folder up of a letter in the world,' he writes to her on one occasion, 'though I hear that there is a peasant in Moldavia who does not know how to fold one up at all.'

Yet there is no record of his showing any feeling for her of a kind to lead one to expect the following letter written in July 1819 after watching her performance in a new play:

Would to God you were released from this way of life; that you could bring your mind to consent to take your lot with us, and throw off for ever the whole burden of your Profession. I neither expect or wish you take notice of this which I am writing, in your present over occupied and hurried state. – But to think of it at your leisure. I have quite income enough, if that were all, to justify for me making such a proposal, with what I may call even a handsome provision for my survivor. What you possess of your own would naturally be appropriated to those, for whose sakes chiefly you have made so many hard sacrifices. I am not so foolish as not to know that I am a most unworthy match for such a one as you; but you have for years been a principal object in my mind. In many a sweet assumed character I have learned to love you, but simply as F.M. Kelly I love you better than them all. Can you quit these shadows of existence, & come & be a reality to us? can you leave off harassing yourself to please a thankless multitude, who know nothing of you, & begin at last to live to yourself & your friends?

As plainly & frankly as I have seen you give or refuse assent in some feigned scene, so frankly do me the justice to answer me. It is impossible I should feel injured or aggrieved by your telling me at once that the proposal does not suit you. It is impossible that I should ever think of molesting you with idle importunity and persecution after your mind [was] once firmly spoken – but happier, far happier, could I have leave to hope a time might come, when our friends might be your friends; our interests yours; our book-knowledge, if in that inconsiderable particular we have any little advantage, might impart something to you, which you would every day have it in your power ten thousand fold to repay by the added cheerfulness and joy which you could not fail to bring as a dowry into whatever family should have the honor and happiness of receiving you, the most welcome accession that could be made to it.

In haste, but with entire respect & deepest affection, I subscribe myself. Charles Lamb.

Fanny Kelly replied to this communication at once and unhesitatingly. Apart from the fact that she was not in love with Lamb, she had, understandably enough, no wish to take on the task of helping to look after a sister-in-law who was a potential homicidal maniac. But she liked Lamb too much to pain him by saying so. Instead, she wrote explaining that she realised what an honour it was to be offered

Opposite: MISS KELLY as Annette in *The Maid and the Magpie*, Lyceum Theatre: tinsel picture, c. 1815. Tinsel portraits of actors were a popular art form that flourished between about 1820 and 1850 and were in their heyday during the last years of Charles Lamb's life. Tinsel portraits of actresses were rare, and this example indicates the fame that Fanny Kelly achieved.

MISS KELLY, as ANNETTE, in the MAID & MAGPIE.

marriage by a man of his intellectual distinction, but that she must refuse because for many years she had been in love with someone else. She added that she hoped that the subject would never again be mentioned between them. Whether her excuse was true we do not know: but Lamb accepted it. He answered immediately in a note whose tone, in contrast with that of his proposal, was lighthearted and even frivolous as if he was alarmed that any note of seriousness would kill their friendship.

> Your injunctions shall be obeyed to a tittle. I feel myself in a lackadaisacal no-how-ish kind of a humour. I believe it is the rain, or something. I had thought to have written seriously, but I fancy I succeed best in epistles of mere fun; puns & that nonsense. You will be good friends with us, will you not? let what has past 'break no bones' between us . . .

Lamb need not have worried. Fanny Kelly took him at his word and remained a frequent and friendly visitor. Lamb was observed sometimes to hover round her with a look of admiration on his countenance; but it seems probable that looking was enough to satisfy him. He had never been a man of strong sexual passions. If he had, her presence after her refusal would have caused him more pain than pleasure. All the same, it must have been feeling, not reason, that had prompted him to propose. Reason surely would have told him that she would reject him. How could he expect that a young actress at the peak of success should abandon her career in order to marry a middle-aged city clerk, skinny, stammering and cumbered with the per-

Opposite: ST. JOHN'S COLLEGE, CAMBRIDGE, THE GARDENS: aquatint by R. Reeve after F. Mackenzie, in Ackermann's *The University of Cambridge*, 1815. On August 20, 1815, Mary Lamb wrote to Sarah Hutchinson: 'In my life I never spent so many pleasant hours together as I did in Cambridge I like St. John's College best'.

manent care of an mentally afflicted sister? It is likely that the feeling prompting his proposal rose from the fact that though no man of passion, he was also no born bachelor. Circumstances had forced him to live a bachelor life but, as his daydreams showed, his nature had always yearned to find fulfilment in a happy family life with wife and children. Can it be that now, with the passing of the years, he suddenly felt that, if he was ever to achieve such a life, it must be by marrying soon. Then why not marry his old friend, delightful Fanny Kelly? Anyhow there was no harm in asking her. On an impulse, he sat down and wrote his letter of proposal. If she refused, he was no worse off than before.

[IV]

What did Mary think of the matter? On this question, also, history is tantalisingly silent. But I doubt that she would have been opposed to the marriage. She was in favour of anything likely to make Charles happy and, for herself, she liked Fanny Kelly. Further, she, too, was attracted by the idea of a life with children. The proof of this came a year later. In June 1820 the Lambs' took their summer holidays at Cambridge. There, at the house of a friend, they met a pleasant, shy man of Italian extraction called Charles Isola who held the position of Bedell of Cambridge University and was a widowed father of a family of children. With one of these, an olive-skinned, dark-haired little girl called Emma, the Lambs made great friends: so much so that they later invited her to spend the following Christmas with them in London. The visit was a great success; both brother and sister discovered that they much enjoyed having a child in the house, though Charles now and again had gently to reproach Emma for dog-earing the pages of his books. But he liked reading with her, joking with her, and taking her to the pantomime. Emma repaid the Lambs by the obvious pleasure she took in these activities; she also laughed heartily at Charles's jokes. In consequence this visit was the first of many. They became frequent and regular events in the Lambs' life. More and more they seem to have taken Emma over; so that when in 1823 Mr. Isola died it seemed natural that they should more or less adopt her. In term time she boarded at a school in Dulwich; her holidays she spent with the Lambs. By this time they were both very fond of her. The tales in *Mrs Leicester's School* showed both had always been interested in children. Mary's letters of advice to young girls indicate that there was in her a great deal of maternal instinct unfulfilled, and this expressed itself in a loving relationship to Emma. As for Charles, he spoke of her to his friends as 'a silent little brown girl who runs about the house in the Christmas holidays' and 'is a girl of gold'. Emma does sound very likeable: sweet-tempered, humorous and with the intelligence and imagination to appreciate the talk at her adopted home and, as she grew older, agreeably to take part in it. Charles was later to describe her as one of the best female talkers he knew.

From the first both he and Mary found themselves enjoying the pleasures of parentage and ready enough to accept its responsibilities. They supervised Emma's education and planned for her future. She was to earn her living as a governess, the only profession open in those days to a girl in her position. Charles and Mary did all they could to prepare her to be an efficient one, and when the time came took pains to see that she got a place with people who would treat her well. Meanwhile, during her first years with them, the spirits of both were raised by the presence of a child in the house. Charles in particular found playing and talking with her both cheering and tranquilising: cheering because it provided an outlet for the strain of childishness that had never been eradicated from his nature, tranquilising in that it soothed him to be with someone too young to be aware of the dark cloud that shadowed his life. Not that Emma can have been for long wholly unaware of it. Mary was sometimes mysteriously away from the house and Emma must have begun to at least suspect the reason for her absence. At first, however, the presence of a child, innocent, ignorant and carefree, added yet another incongruous element to the strange blend of the homely and the eerie which composed the atmosphere pervading the Lambs' household.

[v]

Charles's dreams of a happy family life – if he had ever seriously cherished them – were not to be realised, even with the help of Emma.

The same was not true of his literary aspirations. These first years of the 1820's were to be the most important of his life; for in them his genius as a writer was at last to find fulfilment. This came about unexpectedly and almost by chance. December 1820 saw the appearance of a new periodical called *The London Magazine*. It contained a short piece written by Charles Lamb under the pseudonym of Elia, and inspired by his youthful experiences as a clerk employed by the South-Sea Company. This was liked enough for the editor to ask for another contribution of the same kind. Lamb, pleased to add to his income in this way, agreed: his contributions were to become regular and popular features of the magazine. In 1823 he had written enough of them to issue a collected volume entitled *Elia: Essays which have appeared under that Signature in the London Magazine*. By the time this appeared, he had established a reputation as a delightful and distinguished author. At last he had discovered a mode in which his artistic impulse – his individual imaginative vision and sense of words – could express itself.

It was not a new mode. Introduced by Addison and Steele, the occasional essay, a brief prose piece in which the author discoursed on life and manners and books in a familiar conversational tone, had been a conspicuous feature of periodical journalism for over a hundred years; and in Lamb's own time some of Hazlitt's and Hunt's best work already had taken the form of occasional essays. These, however, differed from those of other predecessors in one significant respect. Addison and Steele, for all their conversational manner, presented

themselves before their readers less as individuals than as representat-
ives of the society they were members of: they voiced views generally
agreed upon by those they would have called 'men of sense and taste'.
In contrast Hazlitt and Leigh Hunt did not set up to speak for anyone
but themselves. As children of the Romantic Movement, they were
before all things individualists who took it as a first obligation
truthfully and uncompromisingly to express their own personal
thoughts and feelings; they used the occasional essay as a means of
doing so. Charles Lamb, too; and even more so. Hazlitt's and Hunt's
thoughts, though always and aggressively their own, were sometimes
exercised on impersonal subjects, such as political or critical
principles and with the purpose of arriving at conclusions which they
wanted others to agree with. Lamb was not interested in general
principles; nor was he concerned to persuade his readers to agree with
him about anything. The essays of Elia were of various kinds; they
include reminiscences, character sketches, fantasies, literary appreciation: but all are alike in that openly and admittedly they are records
concerned only to express the author's private and personal reactions.
To record such reactions was Lamb's inspiration, the impulse that
fired his creative genius to activity. The other literary forms he had
tried had been unable to do this. Drama and stories could express the
author's personal reactions only by implication, not directly; poetry
was a form appropriate only to convey reactions lyrical enough to
need the heightened form of verse for their expression. The
occasional essay, on the other hand, was openly personal in form and
loose enough to accommodate every sort of thought and feeling – light
and serious, prosaic or poetic – that the author thought might add
something to the portrait which was his subject. For the book called
Elia is primarily a portrait of its supposed author, with his views
included only in so far as they make the portrait more alive and
characteristic.

Is it a portrait of Charles Lamb himself? Not exactly: Lamb said it
was not. 'Let no one receive these narratives of Elia for true records.'

he wrote. 'They are in truth but shadows of fact – verisimilitudes not verities – or sitting but upon the remote edges and outskirts of history.'

To turn from Lamb's essays to his letters is to realise the truth of this. Elia differs from Charles Lamb in some important respects. He shows little sign of that gift for straightforward objective literary criticism that appears in Lamb's letters to Wordsworth: nor of that intense capacity for love, and for the suffering that love can bring with it, that declares itself when he is writing to Coleridge about Mary's madness. Both would be out of keeping with the relaxed, half-humorous, half-pensive mood in which the essays are conceived. Lamb's aim is to create a work of art, a portrait whose subject is a man he calls Elia. Elia's personality is not fully identified with his own, though it is composed of elements selected from himself. Even when Lamb's subject is drawn from his own experience he sometimes alters it for the sake of artistic effect. For example, he wrote two accounts of life at Christ's Hospital; one an Elia essay, the other a straight piece of autobiography. In the Elia essay he deliberately dims the lights and darkens the shadow of his picture in order to make it more effectively horrifying and pathetic. Again, in the two pieces entitled 'Confessions of a Drunkard', and 'The Superannuated Man', Lamb makes use of material drawn from his own experience but blends it cunningly with inventions of his own so as to intensify the effect he wishes to produce. Yet the Elia personality is not less real because it is partly fictional. Paradoxically it is more so; and with a peculiarly compelling and intimate reality. This is because Elia is not just another name for Charles Lamb, but that of a creation imbued with the intensified vitality of imaginative art and with something of the heightened individuality of a great character of fiction like Falstaff or Don Quixote. Elia, then, is not the whole and unedited Charles Lamb; but he is Lamb at his most characteristic, and composed of those elements in his personality which particularly distinguish him from other people; and with these heightened and lit up by the light of his creative vision: his feeling for personalities and places, especially for London, his sense of the past, historic or personal, the pleasure he took in reading and theatre-going, and eating and drinking; also his taste for the odd and fantastic, whether exhibited in a seventeenth-century sermon or in the eccentricities of a schoolmaster who had taught him at Christ's Hospital. Elia is much concerned with such memories: he delights to recall his youth and childhood, describing people and incidents in them in vivid detail but as they appeared to be in later life, as seen through a many-coloured complex atmosphere of mature reflection and of sentimental or amused reminiscence.

For Elia's prevailing mood – and here it is most characteristically that of Lamb – is a mixed, rainbow mood, shifting continually and unexpectedly from homely to fanciful, prosaic to poetic, flippant to pensive, melancholy to humorous, and this with a humour which itself varies continually in type and tone. Sometimes it is sharply and satirically observant of human weakness and folly, as when he describes the visit of an uninvited poor relation, apologetic and servile, and the mingled feelings of embarrassment and irritation and guilt which he arouses in Elia: more often it is exuberant and puckish as in the comments he makes on the startling ugliness of an imagined acquaintance of his whom he calls Mrs. Conrady.

> We are convinced that true ugliness, no less than is affirmed of true beauty, is the result of harmony. Like that, too, it reigns without a competitor. No one ever saw Mrs. Conrady without pronouncing her to be the plainest woman that he ever met with in the course of his life. The first time that you are indulged with a sight of her face is an era in your existence ever after. You are glad to have seen it – like Stonehenge. No one can pretend to forget it. No one ever apologized to her for meeting her in the street on such a day and not knowing her; the pretext would be too bare. Nobody can mistake her for another. Nobody can say of her, 'I think I have seen that face somewhere, but I cannot call to mind where.'

Or again his humour can emerge in an unexpected mischievous change of tone, as in his meditations about the different times and circumstances in which he prefers to read different great authors:

> Milton almost requires a solemn service of music to be played before you enter upon him. But he brings his music, to which, who listens had need bring docile thoughts and purged ears.
>
> Winter evenings – the world shut out – with less of ceremony gentle Shakespeare enters. At such a season *The Tempest*, or his own *Winter's Tale* . . .
>
> I should not care to be caught in the serious avenues of some cathedral alone, and reading *Candide*.

Here the tone modulates from romantic to impish. But, as often, it may modulate from impish to romantic, or to pathetic; the pathos of the fable entitled 'The Child Angel', winged but lame, or of 'Dream Children' in which for a brief wistful moment Elia allows himself to conjure up in fancy a vision of the little son and daughter that might have been his, had he married.

> While I stood gazing, both the children gradually grew fainter to my view, receding, and still receding, till nothing at last but two mournful features were seen in the uttermost distance, which, without speech, strangely impressed upon me the effects of speech: . . . 'We are nothing; less than nothing, and dreams. We are only what might have been, and must wait upon the tedious shores of Lethe millions of ages before we have existence and a name' – and immediately awaking, I found myself quietly seated in my bachelor arm-chair, where I had fallen asleep . . .

In the essay called 'New Year's Eve', though still in a tone touched with playfulness, he strikes a more poignant note; for here he is indulging in no wistful fancy but facing, if only for an instant, the sad inevitable transience of all things mortal and in particular of those homely human pleasures that meant so much to him.

Not childhood alone, but the young man till thirty, never feels practically that he is mortal. He knows it indeed, and, if need were, he could preach a homily on the fragility of life; but he brings it not home to himself, any more than in a hot June we can appropriate to our imagination the freezing days of December. But now (shall I confess a truth?) I feel these audits but too powerfully. I begin to count the probabilities of my duration, and to grudge at the expenditure of moments and shortest periods, like misers' farthings. In proportion as the years both lessen and shorten, I set more count upon their periods, and would fain lay my ineffectual finger upon the spoke of the great wheel . . . I care not to be carried with the tide that smoothly bears human life to eternity; and reluct at the inevitable course of destiny. I am in love with this green earth – the face of town and country – the unspeakable rural solitudes, and the sweet security of streets. I would set up my tabernacle here. I am content to stand still at the age to which I am arrived – I and my friends – to be no younger, no richer, no handsomer. I do not want to be weaned by age; or drop, like mellow fruit, as they say, into the grave. Any alteration, on this earth of mine, in diet or in lodging, puzzles and discomposes me. My household gods plant a terrible fixed foot, and are not rooted up without blood. They do not willingly seek Lavinian shores. A new state of being staggers me.

Sun, and sky, and breeze, and solitary walks, and Summer holidays, and the greenness of fields, and the delicious juices of meats and fishes, and society, and the cheerful glass, and candle-light, and fireside conversations, and innocent vanities, and jests, and *irony itself* – do these things go out with life?

The word 'irony' is here printed in italics as if to show that for Elia

ELIA: caricature by Daniel Maclise in *Fraser's Magazine*, 1835

it is the most precious of all the things that death would take from him. Indeed Lamb's irony pervades and permeates the Elia mood: irony it is that, more than anything else, gives unity and perspective to his vision of life. It brings with it generally the incidental advantage of keeping his sentiment from becoming sickly. One must say 'generally'; for now and again Lamb is sentimental in the bad sense of the word, too obviously out to touch the reader's heart and failing to do so in consequence. Similarly with his humour: partly to please himself, partly from an anxiety to make his reader smile, he can overdo his jokes and makes them go on too long, with the result that the reader remains unsmiling. Lamb, very much a Romantic artist, was not immune from the besetting Romantic vices – lack of restraint, uncertain taste, an inclination to overdo his effects. The result is that there are moments when his sentiment lapses into sentimentality and his humour into facetiousness. At his best, however, he resists this inclination: his irony checks him from growing sentimental and he has a lightness of touch, both in humour and pathos, which allows him to take risks disastrous to most writers.

He is further saved from disaster by the art with which he presents his material. This shows itself in his sense of form. At first sight Elia's essays appear irregular and inconsequent. In fact their pattern is integrated and single. But this integrity, this singleness is not, like that of a classical building, logical and symmetrical: rather it resembles that of a tree that springs up, throwing out branch and leaf and blossom freely and unsymmetrically from a central trunk, so that in spite of apparent irregularity its parts are vitally connected with a central principle of growth. The essay entitled 'The Old Benchers of the Inner Temple' gives an admirable example of this. It opens with a quiet conversational account of the place and its inhabitants as Lamb first remembered them and how they stirred his childish fancy: this leads into a more general meditation about the value of the imagination and its power to glorify common experience in a child's mind, which rises gradually to an impassioned peroration:

> Fantastic forms, whither are ye fled? Or, if the like of you exist, why exist they no more for me? Ye inexplicable, half-understood appearances, why comes in reason to tear away the preternatural mist, bright or gloomy, that enshrouded you? Why make ye so sorry a figure in my relation, who made up to me – to my childish eyes – the mythology of the Temple? In those days I saw Gods, as

'old men covered with a mantle,' walking upon the earth. Let the dreams of classic idolatry perish – extinct be the fairies and fairy trumpery of legendary fabling – in the heart of childhood there will for ever spring up a well of innocent or wholesome superstition; the seeds of exaggeration will be busy there, and vital – from everyday forms educing the unknown and the uncommon. In that little Goshen there will be light when the grown world flounders about in the darkness of sense and materiality. While childhood, and while dreams, reducing childhood, shall be left, imagination shall not have spread her holy wings totally to fly the earth.

A less sensitive and skilful artist would have stopped here; but Lamb realises that the mood of the peroration is too far removed from that of the essay's opening to harmonize with it. Therefore in the last two pages he gently modulates back into the tone of quiet reminiscence in which the essay opened.

This quotation also illustrates the manner in which his style mirrors his spirit. Basically it is a conversational, serviceable eighteenth-century prose. But its plain texture is embroidered all over with the verbal flourishes and flowers that Lamb had learned to love and admire in the works of seventeenth-century stylists like Richard Burton, Jeremy Taylor and Sir Thomas Browne.

'Damn the age;' he once said, 'I will write for Antiquity!' So he would sometimes say 'thou' instead of 'you', and 'methinks' instead of 'I think': he had a liking for obsolete words like 'nigritude' meaning blackness: he would revive an old use like the verb 'reluct' – 'I reluct against my inevitable destiny;' he encrusts his descriptions of prosaic contemporary London life with recondite biblical and classical allusions. Described like this, Lamb's style does sound as if it must be disagreeably affected and mannered; and it is true that it is artificial in the original and literal sense of the word. Lamb does not, that is to say, write as anyone would spontaneously speak. But to do so would not have conveyed his meaning. Dr. Johnson said of Sir Thomas Browne: 'In defence of his uncommon words and expressions we must consider that he had uncommon sentiments.' The same is true of Charles Lamb. The unique blend in his personality of ancient and modern, strange and homely, humour and fantasy, could only be truly expressed in a style distinguished by these diverse, apparently incongruous, qualities. 'The style is the man,' said the French proverb. A man like Lamb could only truthfully express himself in a style like Lamb's. He did not always do so successfully. The lapses of taste that sometimes mark his humour and his pathos sometimes mark his style too. But, at its best, as in the passages I have quoted from 'New Year's Eve' and 'The Old Benchers of the Inner Temple', it is one of the glories of English literature combining a conversational ease and intimacy with a Shakespearean gift for the magically expressive phrase and cadence.

[VI]

Elia, then, shows himself both a master of portrait painting and of the fine art of writing. But he can do more than this. He can touch the heart and set the mind astir and reflecting. This he does, as it were, involuntarily. Lamb is careful to avoid anything like solemnity in the essays: their prevailing tone is light. But their effect is never slight or shallow. Lamb has put too much of himself into them for that: so that, whatever their intended tone, the *Essays of Elia* come home to the reader as the utterance of a spirit imaginative, tender-hearted, joyous, but which has been forced by hard circumstances to lead a life shadowed by tragedy; and frustrated. Now and again, fleetingly, the tragic shadow extends to darken his pages. The frustration he accepts, but makes of it a means to triumph: for, facing human life without illusion and recognising it as duller and shabbier and sadder than his dreams wished it to be, he finds in that very recognition the inspiration of a poignant and exquisite art.

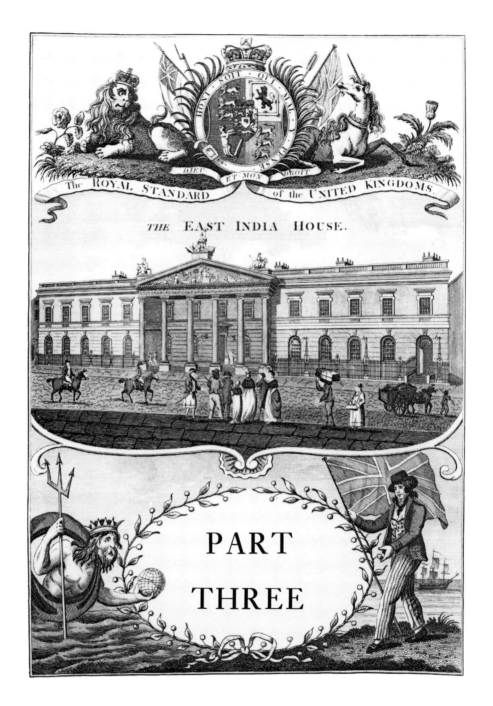

The ROYAL STANDARD of the UNITED KINGDOMS.

THE EAST INDIA HOUSE.

PART

THREE

East India Company document, probably a certificate, 1821

CHAPTER I : LAST YEARS

With the publication of *Elia* Lamb's genius had at last found fulfilment, and with it some fame. This might have made him happier; in 1825 an event occurred which should have given him more freedom to enjoy happiness. He had written in the spring to the Heads of the East India office saying that he had begun to find his work too much for him – he had been ill lately – and asked to be allowed to retire. Within a few days he received an answer granting his request and offering him, as a reward for thirty-three years of excellent service, a generous pension, part of which was to be continued to his sister Mary, should she survive him. On the first day of his freedom Charles wrote to Crabb Robinson: 'I have left the East India house: damn Time! I am all for Eternity.' Crabb Robinson went round to congratulate the brother and sister and found them both in high spirits. He noted in his diary: 'I have never seen Charles so calmly cheerful as he seemed then.'

Charles was not to remain so for long. He was to live for nine years more but they were to be years of gathering sadness. Various causes contributed to this. The chief of these was Mary's worsening mental state. In May the feeling of weakness which had led him to apply for retirement had turned into a serious nervous fever from which he did not recover until the autumn. Meanwhile the effect of this illness on Mary was to give her a shock which sent her out of her mind. From this time on her attacks of madness came more and more often and frequently ended in violence. Even when she was not bad enough to have to go to a mental home she was too ill to see much of Charles. The consequence was to cast him into a mood of deep depression. These moods were made worse by the fact that he had now so much more time for himself in which to brood over them. Indeed, retirement did not turn out to be the blessing which they had expected it to be. It had at once come too early and too late: too early because, at fifty years of age, he was still too young to subside into the sleepy idleness of old age, too late because it was too late for him to be able to embark on a new form of life in which his activities must be the result of his own unaided initiative and enterprise. The routine of the India office had imposed a pattern on his life for so many years that he had grown dependent on it. He had often longed to be free from it; now, without it, he found himself lost.

He would not admit this at first. Defiantly he proclaimed himself a believer in the Life Contemplative: but, presented with an opportunity to lead such a life for twenty-four hours of every day, he began to wonder whether he knew how to fill them. He wrote in a letter:

> I pity you for over-work, but I assure you no-work is worse. The mind preys on itself, the most unwholesome food. I brag'd formerly that I could not have too much time. I have a surfeit. With few years to come, the days are wearisome. But weariness is not eternal. Something will shine out to take the load off, that flags me, which is at present intolerable. I have killed an hour or two in this poor scrawl. I am a sanguinary murderer of time, and would kill him inch-meal just now. But the snake is vital.

He made efforts to fill the empty hours with writing. During these last years he produced two plays, some poems – often written in answer to requests – and a number of casual occasional journalistic articles. But none of these added to his reputation. The plays failed to get produced; the poems and articles left little impression. Nor did a new instalment of Dramatic Specimens, this time drawn from the plays performed by the great David Garrick. This, involving as it did, going to the British Museum Library for several hours every day in order to choose pieces to be included, did give him while it lasted the welcome relief of regular occupation; but the specimens themselves

Opposite: TEMPLE GARDEN ON A SUMMER EVENING:
detail from a lithograph by Thomas Horner, 1822

and his comments on them showed none of the originality and imaginative power that had marked his earlier selections. Only some later Elia essays – a second collection of which was published in 1833 – revealed the precious distinctive quality of Lamb's genius. The truth was that this could only disclose itself in the type of personal essay which he had devised for his particular purpose. Charles Lamb the creator comes alive on the printed page only when he speaks with the voice of Elia. Only now and again did he find himself inspired to speak with this voice.

For the rest his days passed aimlessly enough. He lay in bed until late in the morning and then rose to wander around London, able for the first time in his life to forsake the city quarters, alive and astir with serious busy activity, in favour of districts more associated with idleness and pleasure. Instead of the hurry of Fenchurch Street and Mincing Lane, he now explored Soho with its seductive bookstalls, fashionable Bond Street, aristocratic St. James's Street where his small black-coated figure might have caught the eyes of the blue-blooded statesmen and dandies gazing casually out of the windows of White's Club; or, moving northwards, Lamb would find himself at the British Museum, lingering to gaze at the Elgin marbles whose changeless, passionless beauty touched his spirit with awe-inspiring intimations of Eternity.

Sometimes he took one of his marathon walks into the country; as long as twenty miles a day if he were alone; if Mary were well enough to go with him, a mere twelve miles. One of his new young friends, Thomas Hood, later to be famous for his poems and puns, thought that Lamb would enjoy these solitary walks more with a dog for company. Accordingly he arrived one day with a present – a dog called Dash – handsome, friendly and spirited. He proved to be too spirited. Charles was too inexperienced and too kind-hearted to keep

Opposite: THE HALL OF THE BRITISH MUSEUM: aquatint by J. Bluck after Pugin and Rowlandson in Ackermann's *Microcosm of London*, Volume I, 1808

him under control. At any moment Dash was likely to disappear, escaping down streets, across squares, and paying no attention to Lamb's calls. Dash was at his worst in the open stretches of Regent's Park, where he would often vanish for forty minutes on end. Lamb hardly tried to stop him: he felt that to do so was unjustifiably to interfere with Dash's fun. On the other hand he did not want to lose him; patiently he waited for Dash's return. Sometimes this kept Lamb out so long that he came home exhausted. Mary, noticing this, insisted that he should get rid of Dash.

A young friend called Peter Patmore offered to have him. With regret and relief Lamb agreed. Patmore was amused to find that with a little firmness he was able to make Dash perfectly obedient. Release seemed, momentarily at least, to have raised Lamb's spirits. A letter to Patmore, written soon after, showed him at his most gaily nonsensical, and – wonderful to relate – able even to get fun out of the idea of madness:

> Excuse my anxiety – but how is Dash? . . . Are his intellects sound, or does he wander a little in *his* conversation? You cannot be too careful to watch the first symptoms of incoherence. The first illogical snarl he makes, to St. Luke's with him! All the dogs here are going mad, if you believe the overseers; but I protest they seem to me very rational and collected. But nothing is so deceitful as mad people to those who are not used to them. Try him with hot water. If he won't lick it up, it is a sign he does not like it. Does his tail wag horizontally or perpendicularly? That has decided the fate of many dogs in Enfield. Is his general deportment cheerful? I mean when he is pleased – for otherwise there is no judging. You can't be too careful. Has he bit any of the children yet? If he has, have them shot, and keep *him* for curiosity, to see if it was the hydrophobia . . .

THOMAS HOOD:
painting by an unknown
artist

[11]

Since 1823 Charles and Mary had been living at Islington. Now
Charles began to wonder if Mary would not be better out in the
country. She had come to be so easily agitated that it became more
and more important to keep her away from anything or anyone likely
to excite her. Accordingly they moved out to what was then the rural
town of Enfield. Charles could not regret the decision for Mary did
seem better in the quiet of the country; and, after all, it was her state
that mattered. But himself he could not pretend to like country life.
On the contrary: more even than in his youth he longed for London.
With Mary often ill and himself weaker, more than ever he craved the
distractions given by the rush and animation of the town, and also for
the stimulus provided by the company of his friends. At Enfield

COLEBROOKE COTTAGE, ISLINGTON: drawing by Thomas Hosmer Shepherd (fl. 1825–1840). The Lambs had moved here in 1823, and in a letter to Bernard Barton Charles described it as 'a white house, with 6 good rooms, the New River (rather elderly by this time) runs (if a moderate walking pace can be so termed) close to the foot of the house; and behind is a spacious garden, with vines (I assure you), pears, strawberries, parsnips, leeks, carrots, cabbages to delight the heart of old Alcinous. You enter without passage into a cheerful dining room, all studded over and rough with old Books, and above is a lightsome Drawing Room, 3 windows, full of choice prints. I feel like a great Lord, never having had a house before'. The Lambs moved reluctantly to Enfield in 1827. Colebrooke Cottage is now 64 Duncan Terrace.

sometimes whole days passed without his seeing anybody. He missed London too because as he grew older he had come more than ever to live in his memories; and all his memories were of London: of his childhood in The Temple, his boyhood at Christ's Hospital, his later life at the East India office or, more delightfully, of evenings in taverns or at home with a party of friends. The very look of the London streets, their associations with earlier happier days, could make him for a moment forget the sad present. So did not the green fields and leafy lanes around Enfield. He took his usual long walks through them, but it was observed that his eyes were kept steadily on the ground most of the time, and he appeared to take no notice of the landscape around him: he only cheered up if he stopped at an ale house to refresh himself with a foaming pot of porter. When Patmore, on a day's visit, remarked how much more Lamb must enjoy the pretty walks around Enfield to those he used to take around London, he burst out that he would rather live in his dirty garret in London than in a pretty house amid lovely rural scenery. His exclaimed with tears in his eyes: 'I hate the country'.

Mary, who knew him better than he knew himself, thought that he exaggerated his unhappiness at Enfield; and certainly his letters from there are too amusing to be the expression of a spirit altogether sunk in gloom. But they are generally amusing at the country's expense. He wrote to Mary Shelley whom he had got to know through her father Godwin:

> If you ever run away, which is problematical, don't run to a country village, which has been a market town, but is such no longer. Enfield, where we are, is seated most indifferently upon the borders of Middlesex, Essex, and Hertfordshire, partaking of the quiet dullness of the first, and the total want of interest pervading the two latter Counties. You stray into the Church yard, hoping to find a Cathedral. You think, I will go and look at the Print shops, and there is only one, where they sell Valentines.

THE PARISH CHURCH, ENFIELD: aquatint drawn and engraved by William Ellis for *Campagna of London*, 1793. The south aisle and porch were rebuilt three years before the Lambs went to live in Enfield. The yew tree still stands.

The chief Bookseller deals in prose versions of Melodrama, with plates of Ghosts and Murders, and other Subterranean passages. The tarts in the only Pastry-cook-looking shop are baked stale. The Macaroons are perennial, kept torpid in glass cases, excepting when Mrs. **** gives a card party. There is no jewellers, but there's a place where brass knobs are sold. You cast your dreary eyes about, up Baker Street, and it gets worse. There was something like a tape and thread shop at that end, but here – is two apples stuck between a farthings worth of ginger bread, & the children too poor to break stock.

The week days would be intolerable, but for the superior invention which they show here in making Sundays worse. Clowns stand about what was the Market Place, and spit minutely to relieve ennui. Clowns, to whom Enfield trades-people are gentle people. Inland Clowns, Clods, and things below cows.

They assemble to infect the air with dulness from Waltham
marshes. They clear off o' the Monday mornings, like other fogs.
It is ice, but nobody slides, nobody tumbles down, nobody dies as
I can see, or nobody cares if they do, the Doctors seem to have no
Patients, there is no Accidents nor Offences, a good thief would be
something in this well-governed hamlet. We have for indoors
amusement a Library without books, and the middle of the week
hopes of a Sunday newspaper to link us by filmy associations to a
world we are dead to. Regent Street was, and it is by difficult
induction we infer that Charing Cross still is. There may be Plays.
But nobody here seems to have heard of such contingencies.

Or again and, as often as before, he writes teasingly to Wordsworth,
still a worshipper of Nature:

Let no native Londoner imagine that health, and rest, and
innocent occupation, interchange of converse sweet, and recreat-
ive study, can make the country any thing better than altogether
odious and detestable. A garden was the primitive prison till man
with promethean felicity and boldness luckily sinn'd himself out
of it. Thence followed Babylon, Nineveh, Venice, London,
haberdashers, goldsmiths, taverns, playhouses, satires, epigrams,
puns – these all came in on the town part, and the thither side of
innocence.

Once or twice he went back to London for a short visit. All too often
these visits were a disappointment. The streets and houses were the
same but no longer did Lamb feel at home in them: for no longer were
they his home, no longer did he live the life he used to among them.
The society, which he had been a part of, had begun to break up: some
of his friends had moved away. With those that remained he
sometimes found himself feeling unexpectedly shy. Such a feeling
was liable to have an unfortunate effect on him. Already, worry about

Mary had made him incline to drink more; nor had his head grown any stronger. This led to trouble even in the country. Mary used to ask him to take care not to drink too much at the ale-houses he came across on his walks, and Emma Isola out dining in his company with a local parson felt it necessary to take him aside and say: 'Now pray don't *drink* – and do check yourself after dinner for my sake. When you get home you may drink as much as you please and I won't say a word about it.' This was tactfully put. Lamb came home sober.

It was not the same on his evenings in London; for there he did not have Mary or Emma to keep an eye on him. Though he may not have realised it, Lamb was as much loved as ever. When he came to London, old friends and new welcomed him to their homes. But just because he felt it to be a little strange to be again in their company, he tended to drink in order to give himself confidence: with the result that all too often he ended his evening half-conscious, with his accustomed seraphic smile on his face, and from time to time, as in old days, drowsily murmuring 'Diddle, Diddle Dumpling!' Sometimes, again as in old days, he had to be carried from room to room like a sack of coals, and in the end borne on someone's back to be put to bed wherever he was spending the night. This could happen on inappropriate occasions; for instance when dining with the distinguished and learned Anglican clergyman, the Rev. Henry Cary, the translator of Dante's poems. Next day Lamb wrote him a letter of apology:

> I protest I know not in what words to invest my sense of the shameful violation of hospitality, which I was guilty of on that fatal Wednesday. Let it be blotted from the calendar. Had it been committed at a layman's house, say a merchant's or manufacturer's, a cheesemonger's or greengrocer's, or, to go higher, a barrister's, a member of Parliament's, a rich banker's, I should have felt alleviation, a drop of self-pity. But to be seen deliberately to go out of the house of a clergyman drunk! a clergyman of the Church of England too! not that alone, but of an

expounder of that dark Italian Hierophant, an exposition little short of *his* who dared unfold the Apocalypse: . . .

With feverish eyes on the succeeding dawn I opened upon the faint light, enough to distinguish, in a strange chamber not immediately to be recognised, garters, hose, waistcoat, neckerchief, arranged in dreadful order and proportion, which I knew was not mine own. 'Tis the common symptom, on awaking, I judge my last night's condition from. A tolerable scattering on the floor I hail as being too probably my own, and if the candlestick be not removed, I assoil myself. But this finical arrangement, this finding everything in the morning in exact diametrical rectitude, torments me.

The tone of this communication, appalled, but also humorous, indicates that Lamb was pretty sure Cary would forgive him for his lapse; and in fact Cary was and remained an enthusiastic admirer of Lamb both as a man and writer. Yet a painful sense of guilt is apparent beneath Lamb's jokes: more than ever he felt that an elderly drunkard was a deplorable figure. It was with mixed feelings then that he would go back to Enfield where, dull though his days might be, he had less temptation not to stay sober.

Meanwhile the growing strain under which he was living does seem to have increased his tendency to be irritable if he found himself in company that he felt unsympathetic. This would account for the unfortunate impression he made on the young Thomas Carlyle who saw him several times at Enfield during the autumn of 1831. His description is notable as the only unreservedly hostile picture of Lamb that has come down to us. At this time Carlyle was thirty-six years old, an uncompromising spirit who, after a hard and struggling youth, had recently arrived to settle in England, on fire with genius and with a call to reform his erring fellow men. Most of those he encountered in England seemed to him in need of reform. In particular he disapproved of those he called 'Cockney', by which he meant flippant, superficial and lacking in any sense of earnest purpose. Such a point of view was unlikely to make him take to Lamb. Lamb, on his side, was not likely to take to Carlyle. He had always been prejudiced against the Scots as an aggressive, dogmatic race incapable of taking anything lightly. It was he who seemed to have started the trouble. Mischievously he made jokes about porridge, the Scots national food: jokes which Carlyle took in bad part. Lamb went on to talk about seventeeth-century history, a period about which Carlyle felt passionately from its association with the Puritans, whom he revered as the chief enemy of ancient superstition as embodied in the Roman Catholic church, and also of worldly corruption as manifested under the Restoration monarchy of Charles II. Lamb, deliberately or not, took the opportunity to comment on both these topics in a frivolous tone, treating both as merely a matter for paradoxical joking. He said that he wished Guy Fawkes had succeeded in blowing up the Houses of Parliament and their inhabitants for it would have made 'such a splendid explosion', and that he was sorry that the Royalists had not hanged Milton after the Restoration 'for then we should have been able to laugh at them.' What, if anything, Carlyle said at the time is not recorded; but when he got home he let himself go in his diary:

> Charles Lamb I sincerely believe to be in some considerable degree insane. A more pitiful, ricketty, gasping, staggering, stammering Tomfool I do not know. He is witty by denying truisms and abjuring good manners. His speech wriggles hither and thither with an incessant painful fluctuation, not an opinion in it, or a fact, or a phrase that you can thank him for – more like a convulsion fit than a natural systole and diastole. Besides, he is now a confirmed, shameless drunkard; *asks* vehemently for gin and water in strangers' houses, tipples till he is utterly mad, and is only not thrown out of doors because he is too much despised for taking such trouble with him. Poor Lamb! Poor England, when such a despicable abortion is named genius!

THOMAS CARLYLE: detail of
lithograph by Daniel Maclise in
Fraser's Magazine, 1833

In some later reminiscences he returned to the attack:

Charles Lamb and his Sister came daily, once or oftener (to
Badams' house at Enfield); a very sorry pair of phenomena.
Insuperable proclivity to *gin*, in poor old Lamb. His talk
contemptibly small, indicating wondrous ignorance and shallow-
ness, even when it was serious and good-mannered, which it
seldom was; usually *ill*-mannered (to a degree), screwed into
frosty artificialities, ghastly make-believe of wit: – in fact more
like 'diluted insanity' (as I defined it) than anything of real
jocosity, 'humour', or geniality. A most slender fibre of actual
worth in that poor Charles, abundantly recognisable to me as to
others, in his better times and moods; but he was Cockney to the
marrow; and Cockneydom, shouting, 'Glorious, marvellous,
unparalleled in Nature!' all his days, had quite bewildered his
poor head, and churned nearly all the sense out of the poor man.
He was the *leanest* of mankind, tiny black breeches buttoned to
the kneecap and no further, surmounting spindle legs also in

black, face and head fineish, black, bony, lean, and of a Jew type
rather; in the eyes a kind of *smoky* brightness or confused
sharpness; spoke with a stutter; in walking tottered and shuffled;
emblem of imbecility bodily and spiritual.

These are fine pieces of invective; and Lamb must be held partly
responsible for their virulence by choosing to trail his coat before a
stranger in this way. But Carlyle would have been in any case wholly
unable to appreciate Lamb's personality. Moreover his character and
subsequent career revealed him as in no position to be censorious. He
was later to achieve fame not only as a man of literary genius but also
as a prophet, eloquently urging others to forswear selfish ends in order
to live strenuous lives for the good of mankind and never permitting
themselves to complain about personal troubles. In fact his life story
showed him as a tempestuous egotist, incapable of self-control
and grumbling about the slightest annoyance. Lamb in contrast had
dedicated himself to a lifetime of self-sacrifice without complaint.
Carlyle was to live long enough to read a biography of Lamb
disclosing this. But he never recanted his harsh judgement on him.
What Lamb thought of Carlyle is not recorded. Perhaps he only
remembered him as a grim-faced Scotsman whom he had once felt a
mischievous impulse to shock. It is also possible that he did not
remember him at all.

That he was capable of a mischievous impulse is evidence that he
was not during these later years always plunged in deep depression.
Indeed his life at Enfield had its brighter moments. Emma Isola spent
her holidays with the Lambs. Charles found her a delightful
companion to walk and talk with. Further, though he had to endure
some solitary days, Enfield was near enough to London for friends to
come down from time to time to dine with him and stay the night at
the local inn: old friends like Crabb Robinson, also younger disciples
like Talfourd and Patmore to which must be added another name,
Edward Moxon, a rising young publisher and bookseller from

Yorkshire. Lamb had got to know him first in 1826, and was immediately attracted by his honest, straightforward personality. On his side Moxon became an enthusiastic admirer of Lamb as a writer – he was later to become his first biographer. Soon he was to associate himself more closely with the Lamb household by falling in love with Emma Isola. With these varied companions Lamb was still able to enjoy the pleasures of conviviality and conversation.

He had not deteriorated as a conversationalist. Many years later Patmore wrote that he had during the course of his life met most of the great talkers of his time; but, he wrote:

> I have no recollection of any such colloquies that have left such delightful and instantaneous impressions on my mind as those which took place between the first and last glass of gin and water after a rump steak or a pork chop supper in the simple little domicile of Charles Lamb and his sister at Enfield.

The rump steaks and pork chops stimulated Lamb's conversation: his inextinguishable gift for enjoying himself meant that he still took pleasure in his food. He was too poor for it to be a sophisticated pleasure. He was, we learn, particularly fond of such inexpensive delicacies as tripe and cow heel which he savoured with the same relish as more fastidious palates find in caviare.

Patmore's praise of his talk is evidence that Lamb's mind was not declining. This is also clear from his letters. These were as good as ever. He wrote them to a great many people, new friends like Mary Shelley and acquaintances such as a kindly lady called Miss Fryer, as well as old correspondents like Manning and Dyer, and they were in his old manner, fantasy and fun alternating with sad ironical reflections on life. There is a memorable instance of this in 1830 when many of England's agricultural labourers, rendered frantic by miserable poverty and influenced by the 1829 revolution that was taking place in France, sought to relieve their feelings by setting ricks

GEORGE DYER: painting by Henry Meyer. Dyer had been a Grecian at Christ's Hospital, and was a life-long friend of Lamb. Despite becoming blind he continued to correspond with him in his last years. His dog, Tobit, was always referred to by Lamb as 'No-Bit'.

on fire all over the South of England. Some were set alight near Enfield, illuminating the night sky with a lurid light. The effect on Lamb was for once to direct his thoughts to public affairs. These thoughts, as might be expected, were odd and individual. Though not unsympathetic to the labourers and their wrongs, he was alarmed by the idea – we do not know where he got it from – that they were able to set the ricks alight so effectively because they had got possession of some new and dangerous instrument for igniting them. This instrument Lamb feared, in the hands of ignorant people, might end in devastating the whole countryside. He wrote to Dyer:

> Now the rich and poor are fairly pitted; we shall see who can hang or burn fastest . . . Why, here was a spectacle last night for a whole country! – a Bonfire visible to London, alarming her guilty

towers, and shaking the Monument with an ague fit – all done by a little vial of phospher in a Clown's fob! How he must grin, and shake his empty noddle in clouds, the Vulcanian Epicure! Can we ring the bells backward. Can we unlearn the arts that pretend to civilize, and then burn the world? There is a march of Science; but who shall beat the drums for its retreat?

Patmore noted that Lamb's talk was at its very best when he was alone with him and Mary. As well as loving her as much as ever, Charles found her company uniquely stimulating. Indeed, except that they were both now bent and greying, the impression they made on strangers was much the same as it had been twenty years earlier. Also their relations to each other: Lamb slapping her on the back if anything she had said and done especially amused him: Mary enjoying his jokes but quick to warn him if he showed an inclination to have too many drinks. 'May I have a drop more. Only a little drop?' he would plead. 'No, be a good boy,' she would reply. Sometimes, but not always, he would obey her.

When they were alone they were as contented as in company, playing piquet or reading aloud to each other. Thirty years of hard experience had taught them to live happily in the immediate moment; but it was only in those moments in which Mary was well.

These grew even fewer and shorter. Any change of circumstances was likely to disturb them. One such change happened in 1829 when Becky, the servant, who had looked after them for several years, left to get married. This was not altogether a matter for regret, for Becky was an ill-tempered, tyrannical woman who often sought to impose her will on them regardless of their wishes and whose manner to her gentle employers was often rough and disagreeable. Charles could no more exert authority over her than he could over the dog Dash: and Mary seems to have been no more able than he was. All the same, Becky's departure was more of a loss than a gain. She was efficient and honest, and more than once stopped the Lambs being cheated by

CHARLES AND
MARY LAMB
painted by
F.S. Cary in
1834, the year
of Charles's
death

F.S.Cary.

unscrupulous tradesmen. Without her, they now found themselves
completely at sea; so much so that after an ineffective attempt to get on
with a new maid, Charles decided they had better give up trying to
run the household on their own. Instead they went into lodgings at
Enfield with a couple called Westwood. At first the Westwoods
appeared pleasant; but not for long. Lazy and stingy, they tried to get
as much money out of the Lambs as they could, and resented them

entertaining visitors. Once, when Wordsworth called, the Westwoods noticed that he took more sugar in his tea than they thought proper, and charged the Lambs extra for it. If Charles complained about anything they answered him as rudely as Becky had ever done. It took time and effort for the Lambs to make yet another move, but in the spring of 1833 Charles had come to dislike the Westwoods so much that he decided to leave. The effect of the move on Mary was as bad as might be expected: so much so that Charles made up his mind that it was better to put her into what amounted to a home for mental patients – mainly for those only mildly afflicted – kept by a Mr. and Mrs. Walden in the neighbouring town of Edmonton. In order that she should not feel he had deserted her, Lamb made his home there too. It looked to him as if it was more than likely that she would never get better. A wave of hopeless despair crept over him. He wrote to Wordsworth:

> Mary is ill again. Her illnesses encroach yearly. The last was three months, followed by two of depression most dreadful. I look back upon her earlier attacks with longing. Nice little durations of six weeks or so, followed by complete restoration – shocking as they were to me then. In short, half her life she is dead to me, and the other half is made anxious with fears and lookings forward to the next shock. With such prospects, it seem'd to me necessary that she should no longer live with me, and be fluttered with continual removals, so I am come to live with her, at a Mr. Walden's and his wife, who take in patients, and have arranged to lodge and board us only. They have had the care of her before. I see little of her; alas! I too often hear her . . .

It added to his depression that living in a mental home he was cut off from his friends. From Emma Isola, too; before this she had spent her holidays with the Lambs. Now Charles thought that it was not right that a sensitive girl should spend her holidays surrounded by lunatics.

During the summer of 1833 things became a little easier. Mary grew calmer and Emma became engaged to the admirable Moxon. No doubt this would mean that she was going to see even less of the Lambs than before, but Charles could not but be pleased. He liked Moxon, and he thought by marrying him Emma's future was assured. Charles mercurial spirits rose enough to get some fun out of the wedding at which it was his duty to give the bride away.

> I was at church, as the grave Father, and behaved tolerably well, except at first entrance, when Emma in a whisper repressed a nascent giggle. I am not fit for weddings or burials. Both incite a chuckle. Emma look'd as pretty as Pamela, and made her responses delicately and firmly. I tripped a little at the altar, was engaged in admiring the altar-piece; but, recalled seasonably by a Parsonic rebuke, 'Who gives this woman?' was in time resolutely to reply, 'I do.' . . .

He grew more cheerful when a few days after the wedding Mary became sane again. She remained so long enough for the two to settle down and spent their evenings during the next few months studying the poems of Dante when they felt up to it, and when they did not, playing piquet.

This period of sanity was not to last. By the early months of 1834 Mary's mind was failing again, not so violently or miserably as in the previous year, but as it was to turn out, more incurably: her brief lucid intervals came less and less often. But she knew Charles and she was not wretched. Grateful for this, he taught himself to accept her condition and also the prospect of spending his future with her in a mental home. He wrote to Miss Fryer:

> Have faith in me! It is no new thing for me to be left to my sister. When she is not violent her rambling chat is better to me than the sense and sanity of this world. Her heart is obscured, not buried; it

WALDEN COTTAGE,
EDMONTON,
formerly Bay Cottage,
now known as
Lamb's Cottage

breaks out occasionally; and one can discern a strong mind struggling with the billows that have gone over it. I could be nowhere happier than under the same roof with her. Her memory is unnaturally strong; and from ages past, if we may so call the earliest records of our poor life, she fetches thousands of names and things that never would have dawned upon me again, and thousands from the ten years she lived before me. What took place from early girlhood to her coming of age principally lives again (every important thing and every trifle) in her brain with the vividness of real presence. For twelve hours incessantly she will pour out without intermission all her past life, forgetting nothing,

COLERIDGE IN OLD AGE: caricature by Daniel Maclise published in *Fraser's Magazine*

pouring out name after name to the Waldens as a dream; sense and nonsense; truths and errors huddled together; a medley between inspiration and possession. What things we are!

Lamb's decision to make his home with the Waldens was his final act in his thirty-five years of self-sacrifice. No more than before did he look on it as such, or think that he should be praised for it. 'I could be nowhere happier than under the same roof with her,' he insisted.

[III]

As it turned out, it was not to be for long. Lamb had never been strong
and the life he had lived of hard work, continuous anxiety – and
perhaps the hectic convivialities he had turned to in order to relieve
his anxiety – had not made him any stronger. Now the strain of the
last two years was added to that of the thirty-five that had preceded
them, to leave him frail indeed. In July 1834 an event occurred to put
a further strain on this frailty. Coleridge died. The effect of the news
on Lamb was momentous. He was not grief-stricken. With Coleridge
the 'damaged archangel', a semi-invalid in Highgate, and Lamb for
much of the time out of London, it was long since the two had seen
each other often. But, preserved in memory, their feelings for each
other had not grown less; and, after all, next to Mary, Coleridge had
been far and away the most important figure in Charles Lamb's life,
the friend who had been most closely connected with him during his
most significant and memorable experiences: listening enthralled to
Coleridge as a Blue-coat boy declaiming in the cloisters of Christ's
Hospital; inspiring, fascinating talks with Coleridge till late in the
night in the 'Salutation' tavern; terrible days after his mother's death,
when it was to Coleridge alone that he turned for support and
sympathy; and, after he had begun to recover his spirits, delightful
remembrances of evenings in the twilit garden at Nether Stowey with
Coleridge and Wordsworth in the full flood of their youthful genius,
gloriously discoursing, and finding himself able, though shyly, to
contribute to the discourse. He had comical memories of Coleridge,
too; of his hour-long rhapsodising and wild projects and incurable
indecisions. But Lamb had always loved his friends more if he could
laugh at them a little. Besides, looking back on the past in the light of
Coleridge's death, he forgot his weaknesses. In recollection the figure
of the youthful archangel shone out, wholly undamaged and
illuminating his young friend's mind as no one else had ever done –
incomparably the chief spiritual and intellectual influence in Lamb's

life. He hardly took it in that now for ever he was silenced, and that he would never see him again. At first he could not bring himself to speak of him; but from time to time, and in the midst of talk about some other topic, he would stop, and then – 'Coleridge is dead'! he would exclaim – and, after a pause, continue the previous conversation. Months later he brought himself to sum up his feelings:

> When I heard of the death of Coleridge it was without grief. It seemed to me that he long had been on the confines of the next world – that he had a hunger for eternity. I grieved then that I could not grieve. But since, I feel how great a part he was of me. His great and dear spirit haunts me. I cannot think a thought, I cannot make a criticism on men and books, without an ineffectual turning and reference to him.

Coleridge's spirit was not to haunt Lamb long. Within a year Wordsworth, the last of the inspired trio, was to write the following lines:

> Nor has the rolling year twice measured,
> From sign to sign, its steadfast course,
> Since every mortal power of Coleridge
> Was frozen at its marvellous source;
>
> The rapt One, of the godlike forehead,
> The heaven-eyed creature sleeps in earth:
> And Lamb, the frolic and the gentle
> Has vanished from his lonely hearth.
>
> Like clouds that rake the mountain-summits,
> Or waves that own no curbing hand,
> How fast has brother followed brother,
> From sunshine to the sunless land!

WORDSWORTH AT FIFTY-TWO: painting by H.W. Pickersgill commissioned by
St John's College, Cambridge, in 1832

EDMONTON, THE PARISH CHURCH: drawn and engraved by William Ellis for
Campagna of London, 1793. The Lambs' grave is to be found in the near foreground
of the picture. Walden Cottage is some four hundred yards away, on the other side
of the church

Rightly or not, Wordsworth thought that the shock of Coleridge's
death hastened Lamb's end. Certainly it came soon and suddenly.
Out for a stroll in the morning of December 22 he tripped and fell on
his face. He was taken back bruised and bleeding. A day or two later
alarming symptoms began to show themselves. Mary was in no state
to take in what was happening. Talfourd, one of his young friends,
hearing of his illness, hurried to Edmonton. He found Lamb not
apparently suffering but half-conscious and murmuring unintelligibly. Soon he fell asleep and died. Mary, it is related, taken in to take a
last look at her dead brother, remarked how beautiful he looked
sleeping; but 'apprehended nothing further'.

She lived on for ten years, first at Edmonton, later in London, now
and again her old self, but more often in a semi-insane state, though,
we gather, no longer violent or distressed. It was noted that whilst still

at Edmonton she liked to wander down to the churchyard to linger, as though mourning, around the green turf that covered Charles's grave. For the rest, now and again she spoke of him affectionately but calmly. In the confused twilight of fantasy and early memories in which her spirit now dwelt his figure had grown dim: she did not seem to miss him much. There is a touch of irony in this, considering he had dedicated his whole life to staying with her, at whatever sacrifice. But he had loved her so selflessly that he would surely have been glad to learn that in his absence she missed him comparatively little.

Perhaps, too, though neither had been aware of it, he had, in fact, always needed her more than she needed him.

CHARLES LAMB:
after a model by H. Weekes
from Till's *Authors of England*, 1837

SOURCES OF ILLUSTRATIONS

INDEX

Numbers in italics refer to illustrations and captions